ART AND EXILE

FELIX NUSSBAUM · 1904-1944

EMILY D. BILSKI

with essays by

PETER JUNK · SYBIL MILTON · WENDELIN ZIMMER

THE JEWISH MUSEUM · NEW YORK

This exhibition has been made possible by a grant from the National Endowment for the Humanities, a Federal agency, and through the generosity of the following:

The Morris S. and Florence H. Bender Foundation, Inc.
Oscar and Regina Gruss Charitable and Educational
  Foundation
Alan C. Greenberg Foundation, Inc.
The Hüppe Foundation
Mr. and Mrs. Jack Nash
Israel Discount Bank of New York
Mr. and Mrs. Henry Voremberg
Mr. and Mrs. Louis J. Lipton
Eugene Metzger and Max L. Heine Philanthropic Fund
Mr. and Mrs. John H. Slade
E. M. Warburg, Pincus & Co., Inc.
Anonymous

We are grateful to Lufthansa German Airlines for their generosity in providing transportation.

This exhibition is presented in cooperation with Goethe House New York.

Library of Congress Cataloging in Publication Data

Art and exile.

   1. Nussbaum, Felix, 1904-1944—Exhibitions.
2. Nussbaum, Felix, 1904-1944. 3. Artists, Jewish—
Germany—Biography. I. Bilski, Emily D., 1956-
II. Jewish Museum (New York, N.Y.)
N6888.N87A4   1985   759.3 [B]   85-5613

ISBN 0-87334-028-0

Manufactured in the U.S.A.

Design: By Design

Cover: No. 52. *Mummenschanz (Masquerade)*, ca. 1939

CONTENTS

ACKNOWLEDGMENTS

In 1982, the recently published book, *Felix Nussbaum, Leben und Werk,* by Peter Junk and Wendelin Zimmer, was brought to the attention of the Jewish Museum staff by Dr. Christoph Wecker, director of Goethe House New York. Both staff and board members were struck by the quality and poignancy of Nussbaum's work, and soon began the process of planning an exhibition and publication that would introduce Nussbaum's art to the United States for the first time.

Nussbaum's death in Auschwitz in 1944 resulted in the virtual disappearance of his art, until 1970 when a large body of paintings and drawings were rediscovered and eventually exhibited at the Kulturgeschichtliches Museum in Osnabrück, Germany, where the artist was born. Since then, research, documentation, restoration, exhibition and publication have been undertaken with extraordinary care by many people in Osnabrück, including the above-mentioned authors Junk and Zimmer; Dr. Karl Georg Kaster, curator of the Osnabrück exhibition; Dr. Manfred Meinz, director of the museum; and Horst Vierkötter, publisher of the Nussbaum monograph. Their sensitivity and commitment is greatly appreciated.

In 1983, with the help of a grant from Goethe House, I traveled with the Jewish Museum's assistant curator Emily Bilski to Germany to see Nussbaum's work and to meet the people who had been involved in bringing it to light. The experience was both sad and inspiring. We were impressed by Nussbaum's skill as a draftsman and painter, and all but overwhelmed by this chronicle of persecution, flight and spiritual resistance.

The next stages of the project entailed the involvement and cooperation of people in Germany, the United States and Israel, as well as the staff, board and friends of the Jewish Museum. Emily Bilski has been chiefly responsible for directing all aspects of the project—both curatorial and administrative—and she has undertaken the assignment with extraordinary thoughtfulness and scholarly attention. The exhibition and catalogue provide a thorough and engaging art historical analysis of Nussbaum's work, while sensitively examining the intricate connections between his art and the circumstances of his life. I extend many thanks for her commitment of time and the impressive amount of insight and skill which she brought to her work.

Financial support for the exhibition came from many sources, both private and public, and required considerable research and solicitation. I thank all who were involved in this aspect of the project, including trustee Tom Waldeck, and Renée Herman, Ollie Warmbrunn, Frederick Baum, Hermann Simon and Henry Voremberg, who joined him in forming a "Nussbaum committee." I am grateful to Goethe House for its timely contribution and essential cooperation. Its grant was followed by major support from the National Endowment for the Humanities, and substantial contributions from the foundations, corporations and individuals listed on page 2.

Occurring simultaneously with the exhibition is a series of educational programs examining two issues: the plight of artists and intellectuals in Europe during the Nazi era, and contemporary German filmmakers' confrontation with the subject of the war and the Holocaust. The programs add depth and understanding to the exhibition, and I gratefully acknowledge the following funders, who made possible the educational component of *Art and Exile:* the New York Council for the Humanities, the New York State Council on the Arts, the Gerald and May Ellen Ritter Memorial Fund, and the National Endowment for the Humanities.

The majority of works included in the exhibition are on loan from the Kulturgeschichtliches Museum in Osnabrück, where they are usually on permanent view. The museum's cooperation in sending the works to New York is therefore most appreciated. I also thank the other lenders, whose willing participation has added enormously to the scope of the exhibition; they are listed on page 96.

Each step from the preparation of budgets and grant proposals to the hanging of paintings constitutes an essential ingredient of a project such as *Art and Exile.* Many thanks are extended to the following departments of the Jewish Museum, whose staff members worked closely on the exhibition, catalogue and programs: Administration, Broadcast Archive, Development, Education, Operations, Public Relations and Registrar. Thanks are also extended to the Board of Trustees, who enthusiastically supported the presentation of this exhibition.

The Jewish Museum is pleased to have played a part in the rediscovery of Felix Nussbaum. We are honored to bring his life and work to the attention of the American public.

JOAN ROSENBAUM
DIRECTOR

This exhibition and catalogue would not have been possible without the unstinting work and enthusiastic support of the staff of the Kulturgeschichtliches Museum, Osnabrück, especially of the director, Manfred Meinz, and the chief curator, Karl Georg Kaster. My personal gratitude to them both for their warm hospitality during my stay in Osnabrück, and their invaluable assistance throughout the preparation of the exhibition.

Peter Junk and Wendelin Zimmer have devoted the past decade to the rediscovery and analysis of the life and work of Felix Nussbaum; without their pioneering research and monograph this project would not have been possible. Thanks are due them for their thoughtful and informative essays included in this catalogue, and for sharing with me the fruits of their research during the past year.

I gratefully acknowledge the work of consultant Sybil Milton. Her essay contributes greatly to our understanding of Nussbaum's place within a broader historical context, and she skillfully translated the essays by Junk and Zimmer. Her counsel and commitment are much appreciated.

Horst Vierkötter of Rasch Druckerei und Verlag kindly provided most of the photographs of Nussbaum's work for this catalogue. I am particularly grateful to Nancy Foote of By Design for her sensitive design of the catalogue, and for her patience and good humor. I am indebted to Michael Sonino for his expertise in editing all aspects of the catalogue and adapting the translations of the German essays.

At the Jewish Museum, I was assisted in the preliminary organizational work by intern Shirley Sklar. Eliza de Sola Mendes and Andrea Aronson worked closely with me on many aspects of the exhibition and catalogue, and I am grateful to them for their dedication and good spirits. Elizabeth Cats and Edith Ratner generously gave of their time to assist in the translation of German materials for use in the checklist. Anita Friedman, Karen Wilson and Rosemarie Garipoli graciously volunteered to read galleys, despite their own heavy workloads. To all the members of the museum's staff who offered advice, humor, and moral support I express my warmest appreciation.

Special thanks to Clifford LaFontaine for designing the exhibition so beautifully and for his expertise in supervising production and installation.

I am grateful to Irit Salmon-Livne for her kindness and assistance during an initial research trip to Israel. Christoph Wecker and Knut Heuer of Goethe House New York graciously provided their help whenever called upon. Thanks are due as well to Felix Becker of Lufthansa, Götz Perll of Ringier Dokumentationszentrum, Zurich and Daniel Dratwa of the Jewish Museum in Brussels. I would like to add my personal thanks to those of Joan Rosenbaum to the lenders and staffs of the lending institutions; not only have they agreed to part with their artworks, but they have been extremely helpful in sharing information and documentation.

I am deeply grateful for the kind help and heartfelt support of the following friends and colleagues: Berthold Bilski, Emily Braun, Gillian Lippert, and Stephen Shapiro.

Finally, I would like to thank Joan Rosenbaum for her encouragement and guidance during every phase of this exhibition. Her leadership and support have made *Art and Exile* a reality.

EMILY D. BILSKI
CURATOR

It was about two years ago that I had my first encounter with the work and life of Felix Nussbaum, and that I felt a very strong personal commitment to bring this exhibition to New York.

More than forty years have passed since Felix Nussbaum and his wife perished in Auschwitz. Shortly before the fall of the Nazi dictatorship they were discovered in Brussels and deported to the death camp. Felix Nussbaum's last wish: "Let my paintings survive."

The people and the City of Osnabrück, where Nussbaum was born and raised, were to fulfill Nussbaum's wish posthumously, by carefully tracing and then purchasing the surviving paintings and giving them a permanent home in the city's Kulturgeschichtliches Museum (Art Historical Museum).

In full awareness of all bitterness and grief this all too typical Jewish fate during the reign of horror must evoke, there is to me a touch of reconciliation and a ray of hope for a better future in the posthumous recognition and homecoming of Nussbaum's work. And it is this aspect that motivated my suggestion, that this exhibition be organized in cooperation with the Jewish Museum in New York and be shown there.

The positive reaction of Director Joan Rosenbaum made me very happy. I was impressed by the efficiency and enthusiasm devoted by her and her staff to the realization of this project.

I do hope that many Americans, particularly many young Americans, will visit this exhibition, appreciate Felix Nussbaum's paintings and come to understand the overwhelming difficulties under which this artist had to live and to work, and learn about the rediscovery of his oeuvre.

May this exhibition be a modest contribution to a reconciliation between Germans and Jews, may it strengthen both sides in our mutual obligation to strive for a better and more peaceful future for mankind.

DR. CHRISTOPH WECKER
DIRECTOR
GOETHE HOUSE NEW YORK

CONCERNING THE LABEL EMIGRANT

I always found the name false which they gave us: Emigrants.
That means those who leave their country. But we
Did not leave, of our own free will
Choosing another land. Nor did we enter
Into a land, to stay there, if possible for ever.
Merely, we fled. We are driven out, banned.
Not a home, but an exile, shall the land be that took us in.
Restlessly we wait thus, as near as we can to the frontier
Awaiting the day of return, every smallest alteration
Observing beyond the boundary, zealously asking
Every arrival, forgetting nothing and giving up nothing
And also not forgiving anything which happened, forgiving
    nothing.
Ah, the silence of the Sound does not deceive us! We hear
    the shrieks
From their camps even here. Yes, we ourselves
Are almost like rumours of crimes, which escaped
Over the frontier. Every one of us
Who with torn shoes walks through the crowd
Bears witness to the shame which now defiles our land.
But none of us
Will stay here. The final word
Is yet unspoken.

BERTOLT BRECHT

THE STORY OF A LONG SEARCH

PETER JUNK and WENDELIN ZIMMER

WHO REMEMBERS FELIX NUSSBAUM?

Although I had been writing art reviews for the *Neue Osnabrücker Zeitung* for five years, I had never come across the name of Felix Nussbaum until a colleague mentioned he had seen some Nussbaums years before, and that he "painted like Van Gogh." I therefore assumed that Nussbaum was probably a second-rate untalented local painter who provided pictures that adorned the walls of middle-class homes.

That was in 1970. A short time afterward the director of the Kulturgeschichtliches Museum in Osnabrück asked to see a journalist. It seemed that relatives of Nussbaum's had recently brought about 100 pictures from Brussels, and the museum was considering a large exhibit. As the local press was requested to provide advance publicity, the least I could do would be to take a look at these works.

Arriving at the museum, I found the director hovering about helplessly amid some dozen begrimed and partially decaying canvases strewn about the floor. All he could tell me about the artist was that he had been an Osnabrück Jew who fled to Belgium in 1933 and had been murdered about a decade later. The pictures were now here because they had been brought to him by a cousin of Nussbaum's with the request that the museum take care of them. It also transpired that the museum had previously shown several of the artist's works in a 1955 exhibition entitled *Five Osnabrück Painters*, and that some of his pictures looked as though they had "been painted by Van Gogh."

Sometime thereafter I read the restorer's evaluation, which reported the works in question were in "extraordinarily bad condition," and that "the damage was due to improper storage, the effects of dampness, and the lack of stretchers." Additionally, there were "abraded layers of pigment, cracked and flaked paint, and tears and perforations in the canvases." These conditions led the restorer to conclude that it was imperative to repair the pictures "to prevent their complete disintegration."

As I examined the damaged works I noted portraits, street scenes, and scenes of an enigmatic nature. Many of the pictures were indeed reminiscent of Van Gogh, although some were in a cheerfully naive style and others hinted at the *Neue Sachlichkeit* (New Objectivity) of the 1920s. In short, a stylistic jumble. The best of the group — a large canvas depicting three women, two children, a cat, and some flowers; a strong work in the *Neue Sachlichkeit* magic-realist style — was chosen to be reproduced on the exhibition poster. Some years later, when Nussbaum's then-extant oeuvre had come to light, I was asked why this particular painting had been selected as representative of his art. The answer was that in 1970 Nussbaum's later work from the war years — mature and emotionally charged — was as yet undiscovered.

When the exhibition was being organized little was known of Nussbaum's life other than a few unverified or contradictory — and therefore possibly inaccurate — details. Those of us who were attempting to research his life believed our task entailed nothing more than merely exhibiting the work of a previously unknown but noteworthy artist, and we clung to the fatuous illusion that all that was required was to assemble the biographical data on hand and organize the works chronologically.

Our illusion was short-lived. When the exhibition opened in February 1971, it was a major event. The mayor of Osnabrück gave the inaugural address, and those present included the district administrator, members of the city council and the local government, the chairman of the Jewish community, and Nussbaum's cousin Auguste Moses and her husband, who had come from Israel. The Israeli ambassador in Bonn tendered a congratulatory telegram. The museum's director gave a speech in which he called upon art historians to "give Felix Nussbaum the place he deserves in German art," and the mayor spoke of "restitution for the injustices committed in the name of an inhuman ideology against our fellow Jewish countrymen in Osnabrück and throughout Germany."

The now-restored canvases not only aroused aesthetic interest, but called attention to themselves through their deeper, more universal, implications. Under the exhibition's immediate emotional impact, the *Neue Osnabrücker Zeitung* published an editorial appeal entitled "Who Remembers Felix Nussbaum?" We had at last come to the realization that the rediscovery of this artist involved more than just displaying his art. We had been accorded the unique opportunity to examine not only his work but also to reconstruct one of the six million lives our nation had wantonly destroyed.

Work began. I assumed the task of assembling and coordinating all information relating to Nussbaum sent to the paper in response to the editorial. Among those who contacted me were some of his childhood friends, family acquaintances, and former employees of his father's firm. I received addresses of relatives who had immigrated to Belgium, England, and North and South America. Also heard from were certain Osnabrück citizens with more or less incriminating Nazi pasts, who now affected to have been philo-Semitic — especially in regard to the Nussbaums. At the end of several weeks I had amassed much concrete evidence, as well as a good deal of material that was vague and contradictory. To evaluate this hodgepodge was problematic as well as laborious. Obviously the exhibition had awakened memories. Many of the replies were tinged with sorrow and dismay, and in others the correspondents allowed their imaginations to go astray or had confused names and dates. Did we have the right to blame older Osnabrück residents for remembering selectively, recalling only pleasant times and concealing, or conveniently forgetting, Nussbaum's less sympathetic traits? Although I found it difficult to trace the artist's life unemotionally and with detachment, I was nonetheless gradually able to organize the many often-conflicting details and compare them, thereby discovering tentative criteria for evaluating the evidence at hand.

The first facts had come from Auguste Moses — spokesperson for the widely scattered Nussbaum heirs — who for years had been struggling to obtain control of the artist's estate. She told us that in 1945 a distant relative then serving in the British army had been in Brussels and had searched for pictures by the missing artist. He had located Dr. Josef Grosfils, a dentist, who held Nussbaum's artistic legacy in trust. Sometime between 1942 and 1944 the artist had deposited many pictures with Grosfils with the plea that "If I perish, do not let my pictures die; show them to the public." Although ostensibly a friend of the artist, Gros-

fils nevertheless refused to surrender the paintings to the association of heirs. He rejected all proofs pertaining to their legal right to the estate, demanded Belgian court papers, and finally submitted high fees for storing the works, despite the fact that they had literally rotted in his basement. Grosfils dragged out this lengthy and costly litigation until 1969, when the heirs were finally awarded possession of Nussbaum's estate. In order to avoid further expenditures, the collection was transported across the border to Osnabrück without customs papers. These were the grimy, abraded canvases I had seen at the museum.

Then, in 1971, a local curator of monuments came forward with the information that after the war a British officer had turned up in bombed-out Osnabrück asking about Felix Nussbaum; we thus concluded that this must have been the same British soldier mentioned by Auguste Moses.

In the course of my investigations, I discovered that many individuals whose names I came across (such as the aforementioned Dr. Grosfils) were now dead. These peripheral figures soon assumed importance, however. The actions of Dr. Grosfils, for instance, suggested evidence relating to Nussbaum's desperate situation during his final years in exile, and also revealed the postwar difficulties encountered in gaining restitution of confiscated Jewish property. Insofar as Grosfils was concerned, we soon heard from Margarete Ledel — widow of the sculptor Dolf Ledel (who had once executed a bust of Nussbaum) — that the late dentist had been a collector who aided many artists while simultaneously exploiting them. "He also bought pictures from Felix, at one franc per canvas," she told us.

Since I was on the editorial staff of a daily newspaper, it was impossible to devote my full time to tracking down every piece of evidence that came across my desk. Nevertheless, I was able to outline a rough — and later much amended — picture of Felix Nussbaum. For example, I heard from a couple who possessed a small drypoint etching, *Mill in East Friesland* of 1926 (No. 5). Accompanied by a photographer, I went to see the work. The photographer requested the owners' permission to remove it from its frame in order to avoid reflections from the glass. Hidden behind the etching we discovered a small ink drawing, whose existence was unknown even to the owners. This was *Remain Pious* of 1920 (No. 1), which bore an inscription from the sixteen-year-old artist to his cousin on the occasion of the latter's bar mitzvah. This drawing has proved to be the earliest known work by the artist; it revealed that Nussbaum had made an essay into *jugendstil* (the German version of Art Nouveau). Although a fortuitous discovery, it was not a

1. *Remain Pious*, 1920

particularly important one; nevertheless, it offered the first evidence of his skill in adapting established styles.

Other unexpected, almost accidental, discoveries proved more significant. The newspaper's editorial appeal had been posted at the exhibit, where it was seen by a traveling Belgian art dealer, Willy Billestraet. He told us that Nussbaum had been arrested and deported in 1944, not in 1943 as our small catalogue stated; Billestraet proved this with a painting he owned that was dated 1944. Furthermore, it transpired that he possessed Nussbaums from the war years that in quality surpassed everything then on display at the museum.

During the next few years, Billestraet became our major source of information regarding the artist's life in exile. Billestraet's parents had hidden Nussbaum and his wife, Felka Platek, during the war, and had provided the persecuted couple with food and art supplies as well. After several conversations with the dealer, I believed we possessed full information regarding Nussbaum's last years.

Together with the museum's director, I went to Brussels in 1971 in order to see the works in Billestraet's collection. These works revealed a new aspect of Nussbaum's art, a side of his personality we had barely suspected until then: a man who suffered, was hounded and persecuted, yet who remained optimistic. Here were the works of an artist who — contrary to all our previous assumptions — depicted not only his own plight under the most unspeakable adversity, but who also portrayed similar situations of his own martyred and persecuted people. Faced with these pictures we made an attempt to understand how this man had been able to conceive and carefully complete the large canvas entitled *The Skeletons Play for a Dance* (No. 93), which had been painted in 1944 under conditions that were well-nigh inconceivably difficult. Faced with these works, it was necessary to rethink and reconsider what we had believed to be incontrovertible facts.

The vanity of one of my acquaintances helped in our investigations. One day he came to the paper and proudly introduced me to a seventy-year-old woman named Lori Gittelsohn. Born in Osnabrück, she had fled abroad in 1940. She barely greeted me when she pointed to the Nussbaum poster behind my desk. When she was a girl she had known the artist, she said, and she told me that once there was a painting entitled *The Two Jews* that portrayed her father, the cantor of the Osnabrück synagogue, and young Felix. This painting, also known as the *Interior of the Osnabrück Synagogue* (No. 3), had been painted in 1926, but, she said, it had been destroyed when the synagogue burned down during the *Kristallnacht* pogrom in November 1938.

Fortunately, Lori Gittelsohn was mistaken. The picture was hanging in the museum. How it survived, or who rescued it from the burning building, or even how it came to be included among the many works stored by Dr. Grosfils in his Brussels basement, is a mystery. When confronted with this major early Nussbaum, she readily identified her father, Cantor Elias Abraham Gittelsohn, who had been a well-known representative of the Osnabrück Jewish community. She later wrote us: "I watched the picture develop from its first charcoal sketch to its completion. My father's portrait is stylized, because Felix said that he especially wanted to emphasize the contrast between generations."

A chance encounter with an eyewitness thus provided us with irrefutable evidence that demonstrated how the artist consciously manipulated reality to attain a desired result. In *The Two Jews* the cantor is portrayed as elderly, detached from the world, dejected, and sunk in prayer. According to his daughter, as well as photographic evidence, Cantor Gittelsohn was an open-minded cheerful man; but since it suited Nussbaum's artistic aims, he was depicted otherwise.

Furthermore, Lori Gittelsohn informed us that the young artist painted *The Two Jews* in the synagogue itself, amid the comings and goings of congregants, and that when he painted himself into the picture he did so by means of a small mirror attached to the easel, constantly comparing the emerging likeness with his reflection. It is quite probable that he continued to use this method, as many of his subsequent self-portraits show him as though he were looking at himself in a mirror. In *Self-Portrait with Jewish Identity Card* (No. 86), for instance, he depicts himself as though he were peering at his reflection out of the corner of his eye; his expression is quizzical.

Every time new information, new paintings, and revisions of previously accepted "facts" came to light, I dutifully reported them in the pages of the paper. Soon readers began to complain that since the exhibition had been dismantled in April 1971, the museum had no Nussbaums on display—where could they see these works?

This leads us to another aspect of the Nussbaum saga. In order to recoup the expenses of their legal battle, the association of heirs decided to put most of the pictures up for sale and to divide the remainder among themselves. The museum was requested to handle the sale and to set tentative prices. At that time the museum acquired only a few pictures for its permanent collection. Subsequently, disagreements arose among the heirs and the museum, misunderstandings blossomed, and consequently, a Munich gallery assumed the admin-

5. *Mill in East Friesland*, 1926

istration and sale of the remainder of the estate. Higher prices were then established, and when the museum finally decided to purchase a larger number of works, the prices were substantially higher than they would have been if they had been bought in 1971.

Public criticism then began to be heard, and complaints were lodged against those responsible. Osnabrück had missed the chance to acquire a Nussbaum collection at a time when prices were advantageous. Even though in 1971 the mayor had spoken of restitution with commitment, he had never stated exactly how this should have been accomplished.

Osnabrück was faced with the problem of confronting its own past — a situation common to many other cities in West Germany.

Why hadn't the museum moved when the time was right and the prices were advantageous? The city administrator, for instance, complained about the difficulty in obtaining coverage in the national press for the 1971 exhibition because "Nussbaum lacked a 'name'—he had no reputation or celebrity." If he had been a figure of international, or even national, importance the municipality would have wasted no time in acquiring his work, but because noted art critics and museum administrators had not been heard from, the municipality had no confidence in its own judgement. Thus, Osnabrück missed the opportunity of following up the spontaneous commitment put forward in the spring of 1971 to embark on a long-term cultural program. The museum's director pointed out that the municipality dared not purchase all the major Nussbaums available at the time because this would have prevented other museums from acquiring significant works, thus ensuring wider recognition for the artist. Other voices were raised countering this opinion: the museum should be obliged to acquire only major works, as lesser works would only serve to damage the artist's reputation. Basically, time was needed until the consensus was reached that Osnabrück should possess as much of Nussbaum's oeuvre as possible — major canvases as well as less important works — and that this collection should be augmented by personal as well as contemporaneous historical documents.

In 1975 Billestraet offered his Nussbaum collection to the city for 150,000 DM, and the municipality and the *Neue Osnabrücker Zeitung* organized a campaign to raise the money. The success of this campaign proved that the city had adopted Nussbaum as a cause. Five years later, in 1980, the townspeople raised an additional 130,000 DM for another Billestraet collection. Despite this, however, the works had yet to find a permanent gallery in the museum.

— W.Z.

CUL-DE-SACS, ERRORS AND ACCIDENTS

I came to Osnabrück in 1974 to work in the Muncipal Library. Because librarians are often called upon to assist the press, I soon made the acquaintance of Wendelin Zimmer. In the course of our conversations he brought up his research on Felix Nussbaum and spoke of the many problems encountered in attempting to reconstruct his life and work. I decided to offer my services and assist him in this project because not only did I have the time he lacked, I also had studied art history as part of my training as a librarian. Chiefly, however, I was especially drawn to Nussbaum's case for the simple reason that I had long been interested in the horrifying history of the German Jews during the Nazi era.

Unfortunately, I had little chance of seeing much of Nussbaum's work at the time. After 1971 the Osnabrück museum's slowly growing collection was in storage and there was no permanent installation on view. It was not until 1975 that I was able to view his art, for only then was the collection put on display to inaugurate the fundraising campaign mentioned above in Zimmer's account. Although some of the works were better than others, the paintings on the whole made a deep impression on me. Here was dramatic evidence of how a bestial era succeeded in destroying its victims even before they were shipped off to die in gas chambers. But a deeper meaning emanated from these pictures: they afforded me the realization that the very act of creating them had filled the artist with a hope that transcended his fear of impending doom. I knew that it was vital to obtain as much information on Nussbaum's life as was possible. This was even more important than merely analyzing his paintings in order to place their style and give them a valid place in the history of art.

Zimmer and I began our search in Osnabrück, tracing Nussbaum's early life as well as his artistic roots, placing these within the context of his time. We then moved on to his years in Berlin, Italy, and finally to his life in exile. In the course of our investigations we would have to find out all we could relating to the rise of anti-Semitism in the Germany of the 1930s, the history of the almost complete elimination of Osnabrück's Jewish population, and the effects of the war years — and Felix Nussbaum was to be the focus. It would be a labor of penance and of mourning, and, as such, could not be relegated to art historians, critics, and museum curators, all of whom were then unaware of Nussbaum's existence.

In my conversations with the younger generation I soon learned that despite their shame of the recent past and their strong antifascist beliefs they actually knew

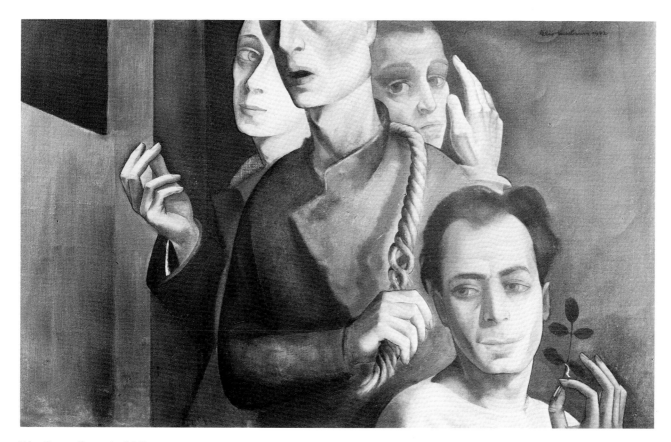

74. *Group Portrait*, 1942

little of the true nature of Nazi terror and genocide. This alone provided the impetus to resurrect the shade of Felix Nussbaum and place him within the historical context of his era. In addition, his work had to be accorded permanent exhibition space in the museum to ensure him wider recognition. Zimmer and I thus made the decision to write a small pamphlet as a guide to the Nussbaum collection, and to direct this pamphlet specifically toward the younger generation.

Unfortunately, the material on hand was inadequate even for this modest project. We had seemingly contacted all possible sources, interviewed all likely informants, and so far no new leads had come to light. As our only hope lay in the unexpected, I therefore wrote countless letters of inquiry to artists born around 1900, asking if they had ever known Felix Nussbaum. Only one responded. Of all people, I received a letter from Arno Breker, Hitler's favorite sculptor! It seemed that in 1932–33 Breker was in Rome on a fellowship from the Berlin Academy, and that he had known Nussbaum at the Villa Massimo. Breker supplied us with extensive, invaluable information, despite the fact that it was tinged with a desire to alleviate his guilt. I was now able

to trace Nussbaum's career from his Osnabrück years to 1933 through documents obtained from the Berlin Academy and from the archives of the Villa Massimo, the Academy's Roman seat.

The woman who was currently director of the Villa Massimo wrote: "Had your letter arrived six months ago, my father and predecessor in this post would have been alive. He knew Nussbaum quite well, and could have provided you with much information about him." I then began to receive similar replies from other sources, making it painfully evident that much valuable time had been lost. To be sure, we could now piece together Nussbaum's life in the early years, before the Nazis came to power, but there was next to nothing about the last decade of his life. Our only evidence lay in his last paintings — moving canvases whose emotional power only hinted at the circumstances under which they were created: harsh years of a stateless artist, a bitter period fraught with peril.

I decided to make an attempt in tracing the course of Nussbaum's emigré years. After anti-Semitic incidents in Rome and the shockwave caused by Goebbels' personal visit to the Villa Massimo in May 1933 (see No.

103), Nussbaum lost no time in fleeing to Alassio on the Italian Riviera. His presence there was confirmed by a postcard bearing the address of his pension. Perhaps, I thought, someone in Alassio might possibly remember the artist, and could give me information relating to his early months of flight from Nazi persecution. After a considerable time I finally received a reply from the mayor of Alassio. He had made inquiries among the town's older residents: "There is a woman here," he wrote, "who recalls Nussbaum's daughter, who even now returns every summer." Another false lead. The woman's memory must have deceived her. We knew for a fact that Nussbaum never even had a daughter.

This was not the first time I was presented with incorrect information. Eighty-year-old individuals are not the most reliable witnesses, especially when recalling events that took place some forty-odd years ago. . . .

After following every possible avenue of approach, I had reached a dead end. With little hope of success, I began to write to Jewish refugee organizations and rescue committees in Brussels. I began receiving replies from individuals to whom I had never written. My letters of inquiry to the small circle of emigré German

87. *Grieving Couple*, 6 December 1943

Jews in the Belgian capital had resulted in discussions, and information started arriving in ever-increasing volume. Letters, reminiscences, even memoirs added pieces that began to form a detailed mosaic. I received facts pertaining to Belgian immigration policy; the conditions of life in exile; personal experiences that offered descriptions of the artist, or which provided clues leading to other potential sources of information.

As more and more facts were learned, our knowledge of Nussbaum's life under duress began to come into focus. After years of writing hundreds of letters to little or no avail, we now knew where he had resided, whom he met, and even how he supported himself under ever-increasing financial difficulties. We learned of his sense of isolation, his feelings of homelessness in a foreign land. We learned of his few exhibitions in exile, and this made it possible to look up reviews in Belgian newspapers and periodicals. We also located several hitherto unknown paintings in Belgian private collections — such as a series of self-portraits reflecting his plight as a refugee. These works also served to increase his ever-growing reputation as a major artist.

However, there was one name that never appeared in this mass of information: the artist Rudi Lesser, who had also lived in Belgium as an emigré. In 1978 the Osnabrück museum mounted a Lesser exhibition, and while strolling through other galleries one day, Lesser stopped short on seeing a group of paintings. "But these are by Felix!" he exclaimed in excitement, and proceeded to tell us about the years in Berlin, when he and Nussbaum were fellow art students, and their subsequent reunion in Ostend in 1935, where they both painted scenes of the harbor in each other's company.

So detailed a mass of material relating to an artist persecuted by the Nazis had probably never before been collected; even so, we were unsatisfied — there were too many gaps that needed to be filled, too much unverified information, too many elements that remained mere guesswork. But, once again, sheer luck came to our aid. One of my Brussels sources with access to high government circles had checked with the Belgian Social and Welfare Ministry and found a forty-year-old file numbered 146129. This proved to be Nussbaum's complete alien-resident dossier from 1935 to 1940, and the contents added immeasurably to our store of information and also provided confirmation of many significant aspects hitherto regarded as speculation. Rounding out the picture, we also found Nussbaum's original alien registration card (see No. 105). Now all we needed was to find out exactly what happened during the last four years of his life.

It was obvious to anyone who carefully examined his

work that Nussbaum's life had undergone a tremendous change after the German invasion of Belgium in 1940 and the forcible transferral of German refugees to internment camps in the south of France. From that time on, naked terror supplanted Nussbaum's fear of being hunted and discovered; yet it is clear that despite this he never gave in to utter despair.

We knew Nussbaum had been interned, had subsequently escaped the camp and fled back to Brussels, where he went into hiding until he was finally apprehended and deported to eastern Europe to meet his death. Yet even this information was insufficient for so crucial a period of his life. It was vital to learn more; we needed to know *how* this man was able to find such strength and hope through his art, enabling him to survive under the most inhuman conditions.

Nussbaum's cousin Auguste Moses claimed that he had been interned in a camp at Gurs, and for more than half a year I made futile attempts to obtain material from the French authorities. But all my requests for information met with denial. Then I heard from a former Osnabrück Jew, Georg Mayer, now residing in Brussels. I had never contacted this man, but he wrote telling me that he had been interned in the camp at St. Cyprien in southern France, and it was there he had met his childhood friend, Felix Nussbaum. Furthermore, he and Nussbaum had escaped together, and he recounted their flight in detail. Another correspondent sent a photograph taken at St. Cyprien (see No. 109). From yet another, I received a twenty-page account on the conditions of camp life, which also included mentions of encounters with Nussbaum; in addition this correspondent enclosed a sketch of the camp drawn from memory. My previously mentioned Belgian friend with access to high places was able to exert his influence and provided us with official camp documents that we could never have otherwise obtained.

In 1978 a major Nussbaum exhibition was held in Brussels. This offered me the opportunity to meet many of my correspondents in person. I cannot emphasize too strongly what invaluable contributions this small circle of German Jewish emigrés have made in the search for information about Nussbaum. They adopted our cause and made it their own. Meeting many of these individuals face to face was a rare privilege, and sharing the exhibition with them was a highly charged emotional experience for us all. Georg Mayer, Nussbaum's friend and fellow escapee from St. Cyprien, gazed searchingly at the works of his murdered childhood companion, while the camp pictures (see Nos. 61-65 and 73) awakened long-forgotten memories among fellow survivors. Former members of the Resistance, rescuers, and those

who had survived years of hiding during the occupation also came to the exhibit. They told us of Nussbaum's attempts to eke out a living by painting ceramics (see Nos. 76 and 77), which friends of the artist sold as their own work under the eyes of the SS. We were able to learn how Nussbaum obtained ration cards forged by the Resistance, of how his hope was sustained through his art, of how his wife sank into ever-deepening despair. We also heard about the couple's constantly changing their residence, and the miserable, demeaning silence imposed on them by an existence lived in attics and basements.

Two hiding places? Willy Billestraet had only known of one: the cellar in the house on the Rue Gratry (see No. 79, *The Kitchen in Hiding*). Even though we discovered additional facts, we still knew nothing of the circumstances that culminated in Nussbaum's arrest and death. With the help of friends, however, the gaps in our knowledge were soon to be filled.

After the Belgian news media featured articles about the exhibition, previously unheard-from individuals came forward, people who had known Nussbaum during his final years. One of them was Christian Jacque, whose parents owned the house on Rue Archimède where Felix and Felka were finally apprehended. Jacque never knew Billestraet and Billestraet had never met Christian Jacque. Until now, each man believed that he alone knew the last place where the Nussbaums lived. The reason for the differing accounts tendered by each was simple: silently and secretly and always under the cover of darkness — despite the danger of arrest by roving patrols checking identity cards — Felix made nightly trips between the cellar on the Rue Gratry and the attic on the Rue Archimède.

Self-Portrait with Jewish Identity Card (No. 86) vividly expresses the constant fear Nussbaum experienced whenever he ventured into the street: the gnawing terror that he would be apprehended by a police patrol. *View from the Studio Window* (No. 80) reveals the artist's limited horizons, the only part of the outer world he could see while trapped in the attic apartment where he and his wife hid themselves — the top story of a house on a street long considered free of Jews by the authorities. Nevertheless, Felix and Felka knew they were being hunted by the Gestapo.

Christian Jacque recalled the Nussbaums were eventually tracked down by the Gestapo because they had been denounced. One night "a spotlight illuminated the cordoned-off street," he said. "The Germans entered the house from the back garden. As they stormed through our living room they unseeingly trampled over newly printed Resistance leaflets lying on the floor. . . . Even today I can still hear the shrill cries of despair coming from the couple, who had been wakened from a sound sleep," he concluded.

Felix's and Felka's piercing cries still echo today, imposing the obligation that led us to trace the course of Nussbaum's life. The search to uncover this life led us down a long and tangled path, and on this journey we had to revise many assumptions we once believed to have been well-established facts. The wealth of material eventually uncovered was more detailed than we had dared to hope for, and inspired us to write an unplanned, but extensive, monograph on Nussbaum. However, we never lost sight of our original goal: to organize exhibits of the artist's work and write the accompanying guides and catalogues.

It is our hope that the present exhibition offers proof of our commitment to this cause.

— P. J.

THE SEARCH CONTINUES

The complex saga of our investigations is only partially documented here. It still goes on, however. From time to time, fresh information is received, and although it cannot change the overall picture, such new facts provide important supplementary details. For example, while working on a similar subject a gallery sympathetic to our work recently discovered photographs of some lost Nussbaum paintings among the effects of an art dealer who had been well known in Germany in the 1920s. This led us to conclude that Nussbaum was slightly better known during the 1920s than we had previously assumed. Our well-connected Belgian friend unearthed an interview with Nussbaum that appeared in a February 1939 issue of the socialist newspaper *Vooruit*. The piece contained much information about the art of the refugees; but more important, it offered a unique autobiographical statement by the artist that provided irrefutable evidence on the dismal plight experienced by German refugees and emigrés in the prewar years.

We have been searching for similar statements since, so far without success. However, we have a letter written by Nussbaum that mentions an autobiographic novel written during his years in exile. It survived after his murder: Christian Jacque recalls finding a neatly bound hand-written notebook among his parents' possessions. He discovered it some years ago, after his parents had died; but it has since vanished. At the time of writing, Jacque has not succeeded in finding this very important document.

We still continue our search for undiscovered paint-

ings. We know that Nussbaum's father had a number of his son's paintings in his Amsterdam apartment. After the SS arrested Philipp Nussbaum and deported him to Auschwitz, his apartment was sealed. Its contents were either confiscated or stolen. Despite an intensive search, these pictures have never come to light, although it is possible they may have gone up in flames during an air raid.

Other works have, however, survived. In the course of the 1978 Brussels exhibition a photographer contacted us and related that during the occupation Nussbaum asked a friend to take some of his more important works to the studio to be photographed in order to preserve at least their images for posterity. Obviously, this involved the daily risk of discovery, but even though the SS made a search of the photographer's studio the canvases were not found as they had been concealed in his safe.

At least one of these photographed paintings survives. It is in the collection of an elderly gentleman in Brussels. It is a pivotal work depicting Felix, Felka, and a young man facing a blank wall on which there is a map marked with the Allies' advances. Felix wears a *yarmulke* (skullcap) and the yellow star, symbolizing his feeling of solidarity with his persecuted people.

At the time of writing we have yet to see the painting itself, and even though we have had several conversations with the owner, he has never given us a logical explanation for the reasons lying behind his refusal to permit us access to this work. Nevertheless, we will persist in our efforts to acquire this canvas.

We believe that *The Skeletons Play for a Dance* (No. 93) is by no means Nussbaum's last work. It is dated 18 April 1944, and the artist was arrested July 24. There are many indications that he completed, or at any event began, another large painting that expressed his hope of survival. We assume it is in a private collection in Belgium, and we are still searching for it.

Although the majority of Nussbaum's works are currently in Osnabrück, many are widely scattered; canvases may be found in collections in Belgium, Great Britain, Israel, and the United States. As many pictures and a good deal of valuable information have been brought to light through sheer chance, we thus continue to hope that similar lucky accidents will result in unexpected discoveries. Perhaps there are hitherto unknown paintings, as well as undiscovered documentary information in New York at present? Our search continues. . . .

— W. Z. and P. J.

Translated from the German by Sybil Milton and adapted by Michael Sonino.

79. *The Kitchen in Hiding*, 20 March 1943

80. *View from the Studio Window*, March 1943

86. *Self-Portrait with Jewish Identity Card*, probably late 1943

FELIX NUSSBAUM: A MIRROR OF HIS TIME

EMILY D. BILSKI

IN 1943, while in hiding from the Nazis in Brussels, Felix Nussbaum painted the extraordinary *Self-Portrait with Jewish Identity Card* (No. 86). Backed into the corner of a courtyard surrounded by a high wall, there is no escaping his pursuers. With one hand he holds up his identity card, stamped with the words "JUIF-JOOD" (Jew) in large red letters. Nussbaum's other hand lifts the collar of his coat, as if to protect himself from the cold or some lurking danger. Instead, the raised collar reveals the dreaded yellow star, marking Nussbaum for persecution and eventual annihilation. At the top of the canvas, beyond the wall, we can see the upper story and cornice of a drab building, a threatening sky with dark clouds, and the trunk of a tree with lopped-off branches. Ominous black birds circle overhead. The bleakness of grays and olive-green in the buildings, sky, and Nussbaum's hat, the acrid ochre and yellow of the artist's coat and star, are alleviated only by a small patch of pale-blue sky and the delicate white blossoms on a tree. These fragile symbols of hope reveal Nussbaum's determination to continue the struggle to elude his enemies.

The power of this image has been attested by its appearance in recent years on the covers of two books: the exhibition catalogue *Widerstand statt Anpassung*,[1] and *Art of the Holocaust*.[2] The authors of both publications chose this self-portrait by a relatively unknown artist because the painting speaks for the experiences of an entire generation of artists who were exiled, hunted, banned, imprisoned, but never silenced by the fascist forces in Europe during the 1920s and 1930s. This quality was commented upon by the reviewer of the *Widerstand statt Anpassung* exhibition for *Die Zeit*: "The artist presenting his marks of Cain: the Jewish identity card and yellow star. Conducting his own identity-card inspection [he confronts the viewer with] a stern gaze, full of questions, accusations, uncertainty. [It is a] self-portrait and portrait of an era."[3]

The sharp contours and stark pictorial realism of *Self-Portrait with Jewish Identity Card* give the painting the appearance of recorded fact. Indeed, the house visible at upper left has been identified as 22 Rue Archimède, the building in Brussels where Felix and his wife Felka Platek had lived since 1937.[4] Yet eyewitnesses report that Nussbaum never wore a yellow star, and we know that he never acquired a Jewish identity card.[5] It would have been suicidal for someone living in hiding to openly proclaim his Jewish identity by doing so. What Nussbaum depicted in this work was not a real event, but an imagined nightmare: an identity check as he moved between his two secret dwellings. Nussbaum is not face to face with the fascist authorities; rather he is confronting his own worst fears.

Clues to the painting's significance are found in the fictional identity card itself. Where his birthplace should be inscribed, the word "Osnabrück" is barely visible: Nussbaum had nearly obliterated it by overpainting. Where his nationality should be, he had written "sans" (without), and covered it with the words for Jew.

These two details reveal the meaning of this painting. Nussbaum recognized that he had been permanently expelled from Germany, that he had become a man without a country and without a home. At the same time he accepted his identity as a Jew.

4. *My Mother,* August 1926

Nussbaum's road to this watershed in his life and career encompassed a journey both geographic and psychological. He searched for the appropriate place: at first to learn his craft, flourish as an artist, and achieve professional recognition; and later for a haven from Nazi persecution. Nussbaum was also continually in pursuit of self-understanding, of a definition of his role as a son, brother, husband, Jew, and, above all, as an artist. This quest for identity can be seen in his numerous self-portraits, which comprise roughly seventeen percent of his known oeuvre. Through Nussbaum's art we can trace the story of one individual and his interaction with the historical forces of his time, forces that led him from a comfortable middle-class existence to the anxiety of exile, and finally to the terror of life in hiding and eventual death at the hands of the Nazis.

OSNABRÜCK AND BERLIN

Felix Nussbaum was born in 1904 in the northwest German city of Osnabrück, the son of Philipp Nussbaum and his wife Rahel, née van Dyck. The Nussbaums were financially comfortable and well-respected members of the community. Philipp ran a successful ironworks firm together with his cousin Simon Gossels (see No. 98), and he was one of the first in Osnabrück to own an automobile.[6] His real love, however, was art and he was a fairly accomplished amateur painter.[7]

It was from his father that Felix received not only his artistic inclinations, but also the moral and financial support that enabled him to pursue his career. The wife of the Nussbaums' dentist recalled that Philipp always spoke about Felix's art when he went for check-ups.[8] According to the sculptor Fritz Szalinski, speaking in 1971 about the 1920s: "At that time things were not going particularly well for us young artists — Felix Nussbaum never experienced such difficulties. He was supported by his father in a manner unlike any other I know of. The father was filled with enthusiasm for his son's art. One had the impression that the father took his son's art more seriously than his own iron business."[9]

From an early age Felix was encouraged and celebrated as an artist within the circle of the Nussbaum family and friends. He seems, however, to have had little contact with other Osnabrück artists. Perhaps he preferred not to risk their criticism, given the total acceptance he found at home. Moreover, his financial security may not have endeared him to his struggling fellow artists — a note of resentment can be heard in Szalinski's remarks, even after nearly fifty years.

The father also exerted a strong artistic influence on

7. *Talea*, 1927

the son. Together they roamed through Osnabrück and environs looking for picturesque motifs and painting side by side.[10] Even after Felix had left Osnabrück in 1923 to study in Hamburg and then Berlin,[11] his paintings of the sites of his city of birth remained within the idiom of the father's own work, as for example in *The Hakenhof on Kommenderiestrasse in Osnabrück* of 1927 (No. 6).

The earliest extant work by Felix Nussbaum is an ink drawing, *Remain Pious* of 1920 (No. 1, ill. p. 10), created as a bar mitzvah gift for his cousin. At sixteen Nussbaum was already a fairly accomplished draftsman and showed signs of the strong sense of linear design that would inform much of his best later work. In *Remain Pious* Nussbaum adapted conventions of *jugendstil* design and decoration for his depiction of an observant bearded Jew wrapped in a huge prayer shawl and standing before an altar emblazoned with the Star of David; this motif reappears in the wisps of smoke rising from the altar. A sense for the emotive possibilities of spatial manipulation is revealed in the combination of deeply receding space leading from the foreground to the altar with extremely flat renderings of all other elements in the composition and the absence of any modeling.[12]

Remain Pious is Nussbaum's only known *jugendstil* work. Another early influence was the art of Vincent van Gogh, seen for example in *Talea* of 1927 (No. 7).[13] A much more successful early portrait is that of Nussbaum's mother painted in 1926 (No. 4). Here Van Gogh's influence can be felt both in the subject and painterly execution of the large floral arrangement at right.[14] But in the strong modeling of the face, incisive contours, and uncompromising study of his mother's physiognomy, Nussbaum went beyond his dependence on Van Gogh toward defining the elements of his own early style. The bold shape of her black hat, prominent against the white ground, and the contrast between the black and blues of her dress and the vibrant reds, oranges, yellows, and purples of the flowers, and between the plasticity of her head and the flatness of her torso, contribute to a compelling portrait.

Many of these features are also present in Nussbaum's first large-scale canvas, *The Two Jews* (No. 3), also painted in 1926, depicting the interior of the Osnabrück synagogue. The two Jews in the painting (so titled by Nussbaum) are portraits of Cantor Elias Abraham Gittelsohn and the twenty-two-year-old artist himself. Though awkwardly painted in certain areas, and strident in color, the canvas is a crucial document in our examination of Nussbaum's struggle with the issues of identity, in particular, the question of his Jewish identity.

Nussbaum's family was not Orthodox and hardly observant by any standard. Though they rarely attended synagogue services, they were affiliated with the Liberal congregation (a cross between American Conservative and Reform) and were among its financial supporters.[15]

In *The Two Jews*, Nussbaum presents himself prominently in the foreground alongside one of the leading functionaries of the congregation, Cantor Gittelsohn. The two men are not really presented within the space of the synagogue itself. Isolated by the column at right, they seem to stand in front of a scene that opens onto the synagogue during a prayer service. This sense of two separate spaces and moments in time is reinforced by a second appearance of Gittelsohn in the center background, standing before the Torah ark, leading the congregation in prayer.[16]

In pose and expression, Nussbaum has sharply differentiated the two foreground figures. He explained his intentions to the Cantor's daughter, Lori Gittelsohn, who has written:

The portrait of my father is stylized. Felix explained that he particularly wanted to emphasize the contrast between the generations. The man with the beard represents the old, more orthodox generation, the young clean-shaven man represents the modern generation.[17]

Felix confronts the viewer with a grimly set mouth and brooding eyes. Swathed in his prayer shawl so only his face is visible, he adopts the stance of an angry young man, defiantly facing the world wrapped in a symbol of the traditions of his faith and people. Gittelsohn, in contrast, has an inward, benign expression, and appears humble next to his young neighbor. His kind eyes look off to the right and his lips are parted, as if he has been caught in the act of speaking or singing. Neither characterization seems to accurately reflect the personalities of the two men.[18] Nussbaum manipulated the images to work through his feelings about his place within the Jewish community. He depicts himself on an equal footing with, and yet in opposition to, a man who represents the Jewish establishment. Rather than place himself within the group of praying congregants, he stands apart, looking out of the picture. However, Nussbaum does not disassociate himself from Judaism. On the contrary, he proclaims his affiliation both in the title itself and by showing himself wrapped in the prayer shawl. This fundamental ambivalence will not be resolved until the crisis of Nussbaum's last years, when external forces compel him to once again address the issue of his identity as a Jew.

Much has been written about the traditional Jewish antipathy toward pictorial representation, especially in the depiction of the human form and aspects of religious life.[19] However, in Germany Jews had successfully syn-

3. *The Two Jews. Interior of the Osnabrück Synagogue, 1926*

Der Querschnitt

Dezember 1933 / Preis M. 1,50

Die Gedankensünde

21. *Sin of the Imagination,* 1933

thesized both their Judaism and their artistic careers for nearly a century, the most famous example being Moritz Oppenheim (1800–1882).[20] By the second half of the nineteenth century Jewish artists emerged in eastern Europe as well. A precedent for Nussbaum's self-portrait in the Osnabrück synagogue (as regards subject, though not the underlying content) can be found in the most famous work by the Polish Jewish artist Maurycy Gottlieb (1856–1879), *Jews at Prayer on the Day of Atonement* of 1878, now in the Tel Aviv Museum. Gottlieb, also twenty-two at the time, included his self-portrait among the congregation in the synagogue. Widely praised by Jewish critics, the painting demonstrated "that art and Judaism need not be antagonistic."[21] If Nussbaum felt that the antithesis between Judaism and pictorial representation still existed, and there is evidence to suggest that he did,[22] by 1926 it was more a reflection of his own ambivalence about his identity as a Jew and a Jewish artist, than a response to any real conflict between the two.

Nussbaum left Osnabrück in the summer of 1922 for Hamburg, in order to attend the State School for Applied Arts. For an artist of ambition, however, the lure of Berlin was irresistible, and in February 1923 he arrived in that great metropolis and artistic center. He first enrolled in the private Lewin Funke Art School, and then switched to the Berlin Academy for Fine Arts, where he remained until 1929, studying with Paul Plontke, Cesar Klein, and later with Hans Meid.[23]

In the summer of 1927 Nussbaum had his first one-man exhibition at the Galerie Casper in Berlin. Paul Westheim, the influential critic and publisher of the periodical *Das Kunstblatt*, remarked that the paintings were not like those of a student and demonstrated "a gifted talent for painting."[24] Participation in numerous group shows followed, as did published reviews of his work.

Nussbaum's production during this period consists mainly of picturesque country and urban views as well as genre pictures. Small in format, they are characterized by a charming naiveté and intimacy; in the words of the critic Willi Wolfradt; "Modest, quiet, pretty [pictures]. . . . Delicacy of color perception and of execution can only sharpen our disappointment at the lack of grander impulses."[25]

Some of these works of the 1920s are of particular interest because they depict motifs that will reappear in the following decades laden with symbolic significance. Among these are Nussbaum's renderings of windmills, for example *Mill in East Friesland* of 1926 (No. 5, ill. p. 11), which depicts a site near the home of Nussbaum's maternal grandparents.[26] *Radio Tower No. 2* of 1928 (No.

8) is an example of Nussbaum's scenes of Berlin life, and of his interest in the mechanistic apparatus of communication: telegraph and telephone wires appear in many of his works.[27] In choosing the benign and picturesque aspects of the city, rather than the squalor, corruption, decadence, and unemployment depicted by artists like George Grosz and Otto Dix, Nussbaum demonstrated an affinity with Gustav Wunderwald (1882–1945), a Cologne-born painter who worked in Berlin from 1919 and painted a Berlin radio tower in 1926.[28] Like the windmill, the radio tower reappears in Nussbaum's later work. *Radio Tower No. 2* also demonstrates his keen gift for humorous characterization in the way the dog's pointy ears and tail are echoed in its mistress's shoes and neck bow. This playfulness was to be given free rein in the series of covers Nussbaum designed for the magazine *Der Querschnitt* in 1932 and 1933 (see Nos. 21 and 22).

The art of Henri Rousseau, so important to the development of Magic Realism in Germany in the 1920s,[29] had a superficial impact on Nussbaum as well. *Country Road with Felix Nussbaum Painting* of 1928 (No. 9, ill. p. 30) owes something to Rousseau: flattened forms, bright colors, frontal nonatmospheric light, and a certain naive poetry. Having tasted success in Berlin, Nussbaum examined the intricate relationship between his art, his father, and his hometown in this painting. Philipp Nussbaum stands with his back to us, observing his son at the easel. (Compare the 1925 family photograph, No. 95.) Overhead, a balloon bearing the inscription "Osnabrück" sails through a cloudless sky.

The pastoral scene evokes the happy memories of Felix's youth, when he and his father would explore the countryside near home, looking for motifs to paint together. Felix stands back from his easel to show his work to his father, his earliest supporter, teacher, and critic.[30] But Nussbaum structured this composition to express his new relationship vis-à-vis his father, now that he had established himself as an artist beyond the confines of provincial Osnabrück. He placed himself at the apex of a triangle whose base is formed by his father and the little girl. Two diagonals, one reaching from Philipp to the church spire, the other from the base of the road sign to the balloon, intersect at the top of Felix's easel.[31] In this way Felix towers over his father and makes his art the focal point of the composition. Within the seemingly carefree country scene, Nussbaum grappled with questions of identity, his stature as an artist and as his father's son.

Recollections of youth and the issue of family ties also inform *Memory of Norderney* of 1929 (No. 11), Nussbaum's first manifestly symbolic painting. The Villa Nordsee sits on the edge of a promontory, partially

15. *Norderney: Villa Nordsee*, July 1932

obscured by a gigantic postcard hanging from the mast of a sailboat beside the villa. Vacationing bathers are depicted on this postcard inscribed (in German):

Feeling of sorrow — which is like a wheel rolling over our soul. But in spite of it, I am no spoilsport — and we are quite a merry company. So let us leave to the modern painters the things that are invisible to our eyes! For today, the most heartfelt greetings and kisses. Your l[oving] son Felix.

An animal skull lies in the foreground and a wheel with a broken spoke seems frozen in motion on the brick road that leads to the sea. Sailboats appear on the horizon where the green water meets a pale-blue sky.

The pervasive mood of anxiety in this painting is largely due to Nussbaum's discovery of Giorgio de Chirico and *Pittura Metafisica*. De Chirico's influence on German art in the twenties was enormous and could hardly have escaped Nussbaum's notice.[32] The use of architecture for emotive qualities, the crystalline forms, nonatmospheric flat light, strong contours, incongruities of scale, and juxtaposition of seemingly unrelated objects can all be traced to De Chirico. (Compare De Chirico's *The Song of Love* — see ill., p. 54.) Nussbaum also employed De Chirico's device of the picture-within-the-picture; the ambiguities created by the tonal affinity between sky and water in the postcard and in the

background are a direct legacy from the Italian painter.[33]

Norderney is one of the Frisian Islands in the North Sea where the Nussbaum family (Philipp and Rahel and their sons Felix and Justus) vacationed. A 1925 photograph shows them gathered there to celebrate the elder Nussbaums' twenty-fifth wedding anniversary (No. 95, ill. p. 83). The family frequently stayed at the Villa Nordsee, a pension that was also the subject of an ink drawing by Felix in 1932 (No. 15). A comparison with this drawing reveals how greatly Nussbaum transformed the villa and its site for the painting. In the drawing the building sits between two streets that stretch into the distance. Other houses, people, and a lamppost complete the scene. In the painting the Villa Nordsee has become a ghost house. Deserted and isolated, it seems in danger of falling into the water.

The whole scene is enveloped in an eerie stillness; despite the presence of the sailboats there is no wind, and not even a ripple appears on the water. Time seems suspended. There is no life, only an ironic reference to a "merry company" in the figures and inscription on the postcard. The skeleton and broken wheel remind us of decay and the transitoriness of life. This wheel — the "feeling of sorrow . . . rolling over our soul" — is also the official symbol of Osnabrück, the city of the artist's childhood and youth.[34]

11. *Memory of Norderney*, 1929

14. *Der tolle Platz* (*The Fantastic Square*—Pariser Platz, Berlin), 1931

12. *Funeral*, ca. 1930

ings that are unsettling in their macabre subjects or melancholy moods. *Funeral*, painted around 1930 (No. 12), marks the first appearance of a number of motifs that will assume great importance during the years of exile and hiding: the high wall bearing pictures of skeletons, fragmentary skeletons strewn on the ground, ghostly figures carrying a coffin, corpses swinging from gallows, and black birds circling overhead. The skeletons, ghostly pallbearers, and the evocation of a threatening environment are the first indication of Nussbaum's admiration for James Ensor. Nussbaum had visited Ostend, the home of the great Belgian painter, during his student trip of 1928-29.[38] Ensor's influence would become more pronounced once Nussbaum settled in Ostend in 1935.

The standard images of death in *Funeral* are self-explanatory. High walls seem to be the physical embodiments of Nussbaum's fears. Even as a young man he visualized obstacles in this way. A school friend recalls his asking, "Do you think I will be able to make my way as an artist? I always see this wall before me."[39]

This morbidity that surfaced in Nussbaum's work around 1930[40] was commented upon by the critic Willi Wolfradt, who noted Nussbaum's "predilection for cemeteries and, even more, gruesome squares. Nussbaum paints gallows and skeletons gnawed on by pink-eared rats; a nightmare concocted of icing and marzipan, a bit of which can be savored in all his pictures."[41]

Organ Grinder of 1931 (No. 13) is far subtler. Evoking a mood of poetic melancholy, it ranks among Nussbaum's most Romantic works. The pervasive tonality is an incandescent blue, "the Romantic color par excellence,"[42] representing infinite longing.

An organ grinder, his hurdy-gurdy decorated with the partially clad exotic figures of a man and woman, occupies the foreground. A young boy in a sailor suit clings to his side. Masked figures dressed entirely in black, many carrying large sunflowers, move about in the background. The figures exist in a desolate, undefined space, which seems to reach toward infinity.

Both the organ grinder and the sunflowers clearly had significance for the artist, but we can only speculate as to their precise meanings. We have already noted the association between sunflowers and Nussbaum's mother (see Note 14). In the Romantic tradition, sunflowers represent "an image of the earth-bound aspiring towards divinity."[43] In Philipp Otto Runge's *The Hülsenbeck Children* of 1805, which Nussbaum could have seen in Hamburg,[44] a large sunflower represents the life-force and is associated with the growth of children. Van Gogh's images of sunflowers, conveying an "overwhelming sense of tough and vital natural energies,"[45] probably had the greatest influence on Nussbaum's choice of motif.[46]

It has been suggested that *Memory of Norderney* reflects the tensions between Nussbaum and his parents over his involvement with Felka Platek, a Polish Jewish artist whom he had met in Berlin.[35] According to surviving family friends, the elder Nussbaums did not consider Felka an appropriate companion for their son and were upset over her recently aborted pregnancy.[36] In 1929 Felix had completed his formal studies and found himself torn between his affections for his parents and for Felka, and this necessity to break with the past, to establish his independence and adulthood, generated fear. Perhaps he is referring to these fears as "the things that are invisible to our eyes."[37] If so, the phrase to "leave to the modern painters" those unseen things, is another example of Nussbaum's use of irony to deal with things that troubled him. Nussbaum employed a pictorial language borrowed from De Chirico, a "modern painter," to give visual form to his anxieties and conflicts. Throughout his career, he would return to the Italian master for inspiration when he felt compelled to express these emotions.

Memory of Norderney was followed by other paint-

13. *Organ Grinder*, 1931

9. *Country Road with Felix Nussbaum Painting*, 1928

In two later works (Nos. 16 and 32), they appear as one of the few signs of life amidst scenes of ruin, and their life-affirming significance becomes clearer. Are the dark figures in *Organ Grinder* brandishing sunflowers as symbols of hope, or have they plucked them out of the ground in order to carry off the last vestiges of life in this desolate landscape, leaving only the organ grinder and his young companion? We are left with an enigma.

The organ grinder will appear twice more in Nussbaum's oeuvre. *Organ Grinder in a Surreal Landscape* of 1939[47] is one of a series of three paintings set in equivocal landscapes comprised of shifting planes. The remaining two in the series (Nos. 50 and 49) depict a couple (most likely Felix and Felka) and a large self-portrait; in all, the protagonists are set within these "surreal landscapes." In 1942 Nussbaum began the *Organ Grinder* (No. 84) and was finally able to finish it in 1943. In all three works, the organ grinders look beyond the confines of the paintings, out into the distance, wearing expressions of resignation. One is tempted to see this figure as Nussbaum's alter ego, a character who shares the artist's experiences and yet who reacts with calm acceptance instead of fear and panic. In the 1931 painting, the organ grinder turns his back on the eerie masked figures and the void beyond them and calmly turns the crank on his hurdy-gurdy.[48] Though the exact meaning of the 1931 *Organ Grinder* remains elusive, its mysterious and elegiac mood exerts a powerful effect on the viewer.

By 1931, Nussbaum was eager for greater recognition. He wanted to engage the interest of the Berlin art world and he succeeded with *Der tolle Platz* (*The Fantastic Square*; No. 14). In a 1939 interview, while living in Brussels as a refugee from the Nazis, Nussbaum discussed the genesis of this large canvas:

But suddenly a transformation took place that made me reach for the large format, because I intended to impart to my fellow men something that must not make an impression only through its theme, but also by means of its dimension. I went to battle against the abuses of the Berlin Academy with a satirical picture that was exhibited at the Berlin Secession and sharply pilloried the spiritual numbness and limitless incompetence of the old Academics. It was an amusing work, which created quite a stir. I abandoned the world of innocence and aimed for greater things. Large compositions were produced; at times taunting, accusing, or provoking.[49]

Nussbaum situated his confrontation between the "old Academics" and young artists in Berlin's famous Pariser Platz. To the right we see the building of the Berlin Academy of Fine Arts, and the Brandenburg Gate is in the center background. Dressed in long black frock coats and carrying their top hats, the aged Academicians move stiffly around the square as if in a funeral procession. In contrast, a group of young artists dressed in white smocks occupies the center of the square, unloading many canvases from a small truck. The dichotomy between the moribund Academicians and the energetic, artistically active younger generation is clearly stated.

Der tolle Platz was exhibited at the Berlin Secession in an exhibition entitled *Künstler unter sich* (Artists Among Themselves). The critic for *Das Kunstblatt*[50] wrote a favorable commentary and noted that it was modeled after Henri Rousseau's 1906 work *La liberté invitant les artistes à prendre part à la 22ᵉ exposition des Artistes Indépendants* (*Liberty Inviting the Artists to Take Part in the Twenty-second Exhibition of Independent Artists*). The same critic mistakenly identified the leader of the young artists as Paul Klee. Of course, the man in the forefront holding a piece of paper (a manifesto or petition?) is none other than Felix Nussbaum, and he is surrounded by portraits of his friends.[51] Many of the paintings that have already been unloaded from the truck are by Nussbaum, including a double portrait of his parents, a portrait of Felka Platek,[52] and a double portrait of his brother, Justus, and sister-in-law, Herta.

Nussbaum was shrewd enough to poke fun at the Academy in order to attract attention, without antagonizing its members; nearly all the members of the Berlin Academy belonged to the Secession, which not only exhibited Nussbaum's painting but illustrated it in their catalogue.[53]

Nussbaum's penchant for the macabre is apparent in his treatment of the area of Pariser Platz visible at right. As described in the review in *Das Kunstblatt*, cited above:

. . . with Nussbaum everything . . . threatens to turn apocalyptic. Berlin's pride: the Victory Column is split asunder, the Liebermann House near the Brandenburg Gate is half demolished. Upstairs, where the studio was, above the broken wall one sees the former master of German art, the last self-portrait saved from destruction.

A line of top-hatted men clad in black approaches the ruins of Liebermann's house, led by a figure with a large drum. It is tempting to read into this funereal procession and the destruction of Liebermann's house a prediction of things to come: the victorious National Socialists parading through Pariser Platz and the dismissal in May 1933 of the eighty-five-year-old Liebermann, a Jew, from his position as President of the Berlin Academy.[54] It seems more likely, however, that Nussbaum was merely thumbing his nose at the "threat" he and his young colleagues posed to the Berlin art establishment. Nussbaum's art was never highly political. Even during the crises of exile, internment, and hiding, all experience was refracted through a highly personal lens. Only seldomly did he refer to his situation within the larger context of world events. The ominous overtones of *Der tolle Platz* are consistent with the sense of menace and disquiet noted in works like *Memory of Norderney* (No. 11) and *Funeral* (No. 12) and need not be interpreted as any prophecy on the artist's part.[55]

Nussbaum's talent as a draftsman is evident in a number of drawings executed in 1932, among them *Fishing Boats off Norderney* (No. 19), *Norderney: Villa Nordsee* (No. 15), and *Outdoor Workshop* (No. 18). All these works are characterized by a sure hand, a bold sense of linear patterning, a sensitivity for the expressive nuances of line, and a skillful use of the white of the paper in creating an effective composition. In fact, many of Nussbaum's most successful paintings seem to be conceived in linear rather than painterly terms. His gift for drawing did not go unnoticed by the critics. For example, Paul Westheim wrote, in connection with an exhibition at Wertheim Gallery: "Nussbaum's drawings

are so eminently accomplished that it seems he can permit himself anything; therefore he is tempted not to be simple, but instead playful, capricious, romanticizing."[56]

After the success of *Der tolle Platz* in the 1931 Secession exhibition, Nussbaum took the next logical step. In March 1932 he applied for the annual *Grossen Staatspreis* of the Berlin Academy that provided a stipend, studio space, and free room and board at the Academy's Villa Massimo in Rome (see No. 99). Nussbaum submitted five paintings for the jury's consideration, including *Der tolle Platz* and *Black Poodle* of 1932 (No. 16) and *The Shameless Sculpture* (No. 17) of the same year. Though he was not awarded this special Rome fellowship (commonly called the *Rompreis*), Nussbaum did receive a six-month grant to be a study guest at the Villa Massimo (see No. 100). This grant provided studio space, free room and breakfast, but no stipend. In spite of his disappointment, more for reasons of prestige than financial need, Nussbaum accepted the Academy's offer of a lesser grant and took up residence in Rome in October 1932.

32. *The Classical Singing Lesson*, 1935

ITALY

The artistic treasures of Rome — Antique, Renaissance, and Baroque masterpieces of painting, sculpture, and architecture — which had lured generations of northern artists to Rome and forever altered their vision, seem to have had little influence on Nussbaum. In the 1939 interview published in *Vooruit* he acknowledged this:

. . . disappointment awaited me in Italy, especially in Rome. This city gave me none of the things that she seems to have given others. It all struck me as so artificial, archaeological, and unreal. In particular, playing with the immense ruins and the broken columns inspired no more than artistic trickery and drove me to roguish literary statements.

Ruins and broken columns will appear in Nussbaum's post-Roman work (see No. 32), but they were also present in paintings from the Berlin years (see Nos. 14 and 16).

In Rome, Nussbaum painted the same kind of pictures he had painted in Osnabrück, Berlin, and elsewhere: charming scenes of local life. *Farmyard in the Roman*

16. *Black Poodle*, 1932

19. *Fishing Boats off Norderney*, 1932

Campagna of 1933 (No. 23) reveals a sensitivity to the distinctive ambiance and colors of the Roman countryside, the particular blue of a Mediterranean sky and the earth tones of land and buildings. Genre elements, such as the little boy with his dog and the chickens, still dominate. The cart, which is only one of several elements in this farm scene, becomes the central motif in *Wall in Rome* of 1932 (No. 20).

Here Nussbaum reduced the number of incidental details, carefully constructing a composition of simple grandeur composed of rather humble objects. The wide bands of color parallel to the picture plane, representing earth, wall, and sky are enlivened and differentiated by the variety of brushstrokes. For the cream-colored sky, Nussbaum used broad horizontal strokes and allowed the texture of the canvas to show through. Shades of dark brown applied with strokes moving in different directions convey the sense of an old weathered wall. The

thickest impasto is reserved for the burnt sienna of the earth. Agitated brushstrokes recall the earlier influence of Van Gogh, but here they are subservient to the overall structure of the composition. This new simplicity and architectonic approach constitutes the legacy of Nussbaum's Roman sojourn.

Two catastrophic events intervened to spoil Nussbaum's Roman idyll. The first was highly personal, the second altered the course of human history.

For the period of his residence in Rome, Nussbaum had rented his Berlin studio to a fellow artist. Toward the end of 1932 a fire broke out in this studio, destroying all the works Nussbaum had left there, estimated at 150 paintings and drawings. This accounts for the relative paucity of surviving works from Nussbaum's early career and explains his future practice of carrying his entire output with him each time he moved.

The losses sustained in this fire spurred Nussbaum to

20. *Wall in Rome*, 1932

24. *Destruction (1)*, ca. 1933

25. *Destruction (2)*, 1933

31. *Sick Horseman (Death and the Rider)*, 1935

29. *Rapallo*, 1934

30. *Underpass in Rapallo*, 1934

work even harder. Herbert Gericke, director of the Villa Massimo, commented on the fire and Nussbaum's diligence in a letter of January 6, 1933, to the Prussian Ministry for Science, Art, and Popular Education, recommending financial support for Nussbaum.[58] Though his original grant expired at the end of March 1933, the Directorship of the Academy was pleased enough with Nussbaum's work to award him an extension through the end of June.

The second catastrophe rendered this extension obsolete. With Hitler's rise to power on January 30, 1933, the persecution of Jews began in Germany. Boycotting of Jewish businesses took place in Osnabrück, as elsewhere within the Third Reich on April 1 (see No. 102), and in May the National Socialists removed their "enemies" from all civic posts, including the universities. (Max Liebermann was among those forced out of their positions.) Nussbaum's grant at the Villa Massimo was also withdrawn, and so began eleven years of exile for the twenty-nine-year-old artist who was never to return to his native Germany. His abrupt departure from the Villa Massimo is referred to in his letter of June 11, 1933, to Herbert Gericke (No. 104).

Destruction (1) (No. 24), was Nussbaum's immediate response to these two tragic events, the fire in his Berlin studio and the Nazis' rise to power: vulnerable and grieving, a couple stands, amid the ruins of civilization. The man's head is thrown back and his mouth is wide open as he cries out in agony and disbelief; broken columns and pieces of statuary — the remnants of architecture and art — litter the landscape; a tottering campanile (the Leaning Tower of Pisa?) alludes to Nussbaum's present location in Italy; the large black windmill is a reference to the places of his youth and childhood in northern Europe (see No. 5). Felix and Felka, like the couple in this drawing, have no place to go. Forced to leave Rome and unable to return to Germany, they bewail their predicament.[59] Figures standing at left, in front of the campanile, blow trumpets pointed toward the heavens, like angels heralding the Apocalypse.

Having experienced the sudden destruction of the world as he knew it, Nussbaum created this drawing, which in its urgency and violent brushwork recalls the apocalyptic landscapes of Ludwig Meidner. Executed with speed and energy, it conveys the fear and disorientation Nussbaum must have felt in those first weeks after he left the Villa Massimo.[60]

In the second version of *Destruction* (No. 25), painted in oil on canvas, the immediate panic expressed in the drawing has been frozen and intellectualized. The landscape is barren except for the ruins of a Roman arena (probably the Colosseum), two walled structures, and a man and woman huddled together at left. Broken canvases are strewn in the foreground along with pieces of canvas stretchers. The three crosses of Golgotha are depicted on the central shattered canvas, signaling not only the destruction of the artistic world as Nussbaum knew it, but of the Christian world as well.[61] De Chirico's influence is evident in the architecture and in the threatening open spaces.

Upon leaving Rome, Nussbaum and Felka Platek went to Alassio. After the initial shock they settled into a comfortable existence, painting sites on the Italian Riviera. Supported by his father, their life resembled an extended vacation.

Untroubled views of boats, water, and beach life were Nussbaum's subjects during this first period of exile (see Nos. 26–29). The best of these works is characterized by the architectonic qualities of *Wall in Rome* (No. 20). *White Boat in Front of a Wall* (No. 26), is sparing in its choice of motifs: a boat, a wall, earth and sea. Closely related tones of beiges and browns are set against the blue of the water. The sweeping curve of the boat is echoed in the edge of a large shadow at right, cast by an unseen object. Lively brushwork creates a feeling for the textures of each surface. The wires of the lamp boldly cut across the surface of the sheet. In these few lines Nussbaum binds together the whole composition. This deft graphic touch is a hallmark of Nussbaum's best work.

Fisherman's House in Alassio of 1933 (No. 27) repeats the basic color harmonies of browns, ochre, and cream, set off by blue, and depicts the boat and fishing nets with which many local residents earned their livelihood.

In 1934, in Rapallo, Nussbaum was reunited with his parents. The happiness of this period is reflected in the colorful views of lush landscapes in works like *Rapallo* of 1934 (No. 29). Nevertheless, the disturbing reality of Nussbaum's situation and uncertain future surfaces in *Underpass in Rapallo* of 1934 (No. 30). A road leads from the foreground to an underpass in an embankment, but we cannot see through to the other side. The arched opening of the tunnel is dark and the road seems impassable. Once again Nussbaum has visualized a wall before him, and he does not know where to turn. A white sun hanging dead center in the sky contributes to the viewer's sense of unease.

BELGIUM: 1935–1940

Early in 1935 Philipp and Rahel Nussbaum, homesick for Germany, left Rapallo and moved to Cologne.[62] Having obtained French visas, Felix and Felka went to Paris in January 1935, and from there acquired tourist visas for Belgium, arriving in the port of Ostend on February 2.

Nussbaum's artistic production during the years 1935–1940 consisted of views of his surroundings, first in Ostend and later in Brussels; symbolic works expressing the anxieties of life in exile and the changing nature of his relationship with Felka, and self-portraits reflecting his varying states of mind and the struggle to maintain his identity under ever-worsening conditions.

One of the first works from the Belgian period, *The Classical Singing Lesson* of 1935 (No. 32, ill. p. 32) is a reworking of motifs from the 1933 drawing *Destruction (1)* (No. 24). The drawing represents Nussbaum's fear at the moment catastrophe struck, whereas the 1935 gouache offers an update on his situation as he and Felka tried to rebuild their lives in Belgium.

Those aspects of their world that were destroyed in 1933 have not really been repaired, but the couple in *The Classical Singing Lesson* attempts to incorporate the ruins into their new surroundings. The toppled and broken columns serve as furniture, and a piece of Classical statuary decorates their new abode. Instead of two stray cats, they are joined by a well-groomed French poodle, a quotation from the 1932 painting *Black Poodle* (No. 16). The couple's clothing is similar to that of their counterparts in *Destruction (1)*: the man wears a formal black suit, the woman wears a speckled gown. The stance of the man has been only slightly altered: the head is still thrown back and the mouth is wide open; but instead of screaming he is singing.

Despite the hardships of their new life, the couple holds fast to their culture, represented by the German custom of performing chamber music or singing *lieder* at home. In fact, the symbols of their culture — the statue, piano, and violin — are the only objects they possess. Thus, Nussbaum expresses the situation of the refugee with few material possessions, who relies on his intellectual and cultural heritage to sustain him in his new environment. During the first two years of their exile in Belgium, Nussbaum and Felka Platek moved every six months in order to renew their residence permits.

This nomadic existence made it impractical to acquire too many household items. Their stateless condition and lack of a permanent home is represented in the gouache: the couple is depicted in a courtyard open to the elements — no roof to protect them and an absence of objects associated with a normal domestic existence.

Here the wall motif is given a double meaning: it not only encloses the figures but also seems to shelter them from the dangers of the outside world. Exile is seen as both a kind of prison and a refuge. Beyond the walls are leafless trees with branches like hands whose fingers

26. *White Boat in Front of a Wall*, 1933

38. *Fishwife in Harbor*, 1936

33. *Masks and Cat (Masked Self-Portrait as Painter)*, 1935

claw at the sky. These threatening trees remain a mainstay of Nussbaum's personal iconography. The large sunflowers strike an ambiguous chord. Whereas by their very nature they seem to be life-affirming and hopeful signs, there is something terrifying about their gigantic proportions. Everything that lies beyond the wall is ultimately unknown. Though Nussbaum tried to be optimistic about the future, it was impossible to face it without apprehension.

Anxiety is also evident in *Sick Horseman* of 1935 (No. 31, ill. p. 36), where gallows, wall, and ghostly figure of *Funeral* (No. 12) reappear, joined by the bare trees. The (dismounted) horseman of the title is still alive and in flight, but whether he will elude the figure of death emerging from a gate in the wall remains in question.

Nussbaum had first visited Ostend during his student trip in 1928–29. At that time he painted scenes of the harbor, and this locale reoccupied him when he returned in 1935. Boats had always attracted Nussbaum; he painted them in Norderney, in France and Belgium during his travels of 1928–29, and in Italy. With his love of linear interplay, it is hardly surprising that Nussbaum was attracted to masts and rigging as motifs for study (see No. 37).[63]

Ever sensitive to the details of daily life in his environment, Nussbaum also depicted the people who worked in the port, as, for example in *Fishwife in Harbor* of 1936 (No. 38). Yet in this haunting image, Nussbaum went beyond the mere depiction of local color. The stooped, heavy-set woman with downturned mouth and eyes, has a face so white it resembles a Kabuki mask. She is hemmed in by the oversized luridly pink fish and the wheelbarrow looming in the foreground. There are no customers in sight, only a lone sailor or dockworker in the background. The street with its rushing perspective, decked out with ominous banners, seems to recede into oblivion.[64]

The self-portraits of 1935 to 1939 provide the viewer with tremendous insights into the plight of the artist in exile. In many of these works, Nussbaum used the imagery of masks to express this idea.

Masked figures in various guises appear frequently in European art of the 1920s. Clowns, harlequins, and carnival masquerades were depicted by Max Beckmann, Karl Hofer, and Pablo Picasso, to name just a few. Through identification with these masked and costumed figures, these artists reflected upon their role as outsiders, the isolation of the individual within society, and the battle between the sexes.[65]

The mask made its first appearance in Nussbaum's oeuvre in 1928 *(Painter with Mask and Palette)*.[66] In one of his 1933 cover designs for *Der Querschnitt* (No. 22),

Nussbaum depicted a snowman holding an umbrella. Two masks, one male and one female, hang from the umbrella straining toward each other to exchange a kiss.

With the pressures of exile, the mask acquired a new poignancy. In *Masks and Cat* of 1935 (No. 33), Nussbaum depicted himself with a palette and wearing a clown's mask. Two other masked figures and a cat are also present. In the background we see the bare trees and black birds we have come to recognize as embodiments of anxiety. Whether this is a view out a window or a painting in progress remains ambiguous. Nussbaum's right hand is not visible, being obscured by the palette, which is not really held but seems to hover in space. His left hand is raised, encased in a black glove.

In this work, painted shortly after his arrival in Belgium, Nussbaum explored the problem of his identity in a new land. To be accepted in an alien society, which barely tolerated his presence, he had to "put on a good face," be accommodating, and dissimulate. Expressions of anger, frustration, or fear had to be concealed behind a cheerful countenance from the people around him, and perhaps even from himself. Nussbaum also called into question his role as an artist. The palette is prominently displayed, but it is strangely disassociated from Nussbaum's hand, and there are no paintbrushes in sight. (Compare *Self-Portrait at the Easel* of 1943, No. 85, where the act of painting is emphasized.) Nussbaum's concerns as to how he could function professionally in Belgium were not unfounded. Having established himself with the galleries, journalists, and public in Berlin, he now faced the prospect of starting from scratch. The question of how he would fare as an artist was clearly paramount in his mind.

In another 1935 painting, *Two Masks* (No. 34), Nussbaum dispensed with the faces behind the masks altogether. He portrayed himself as a mask with a turban, large nose, moustache, and pipe, hanging alongside a mask representing Felka, which is draped with a dishtowel. This is the first appearance of the dishtowel, an object that held a deep personal significance for the artist. Peter Junk and Wendelin Zimmer have suggested that it represents the realm of the household.[67] Dishtowels would have been one of the few domestic items that Felix and Felka carried with them in their rootless existence during the period when they were changing residences every six months. The dishtowel might then have represented their efforts to maintain a normal domestic life despite these unstable conditions.

A blue-patterned dishtowel appears as an attribute in *Self-Portrait with Dishtowel*, from around 1935 (No. 36), knotted around Nussbaum's neck and draped over his right shoulder. Bare-chested and vulnerable he assumes

35. *Self-Portrait with Canvas Stretcher*, 1935

41. *Self-Portrait with Shadow*, 1936

a clownlike expression. Though the hat he wears has been identified as a beret, it is much stiffer than any of the many berets in which he sometimes portrayed himself (compare Nos. 35 and 41). He transformed the beret, symbol of his life as an artist, into a type of fool's hat. The fantasy of this self-portrait is juxtaposed with his actual surroundings, since behind him rise the rooftops of Ostend.

A possible source for the imagery in this self-portrait may be Karl Hofer's *Young Man with Headcloth*, from around 1928, which depicts a bare-chested man whose head is wrapped in a striped cloth.[68] The art of Karl Hofer, one of the most respected teachers at the Berlin Academy and much admired by Philipp Nussbaum, also exerted a strong stylistic influence on Felix.[69]

In the blue-and-white dishtowel there may also be an echo (probably unconscious) of the blue-and-white prayer shawl that Jewish men traditionally wrap around themselves. Similarly, the shape of the hat in this self-portrait is reminiscent of the *Judenhut* (Jew's hat) that Jews were required to wear in much of Europe in medieval times.[70]

A reaffirmation of Nussbaum's self-confidence and identity as an artist is communicated in *Self-Portrait with Canvas Stretcher* of 1935 (No. 35). Here he confronts the viewer directly, his face marked with determination, holding the canvas stretcher before him like a shield. The smock draped over his left shoulder and the beret are part of the costume of the artist, and it has been suggested that the pipe signifies comfort and security.[71]

An extraordinary group of large charcoal drawings executed in 1936 documents Nussbaum's fascination with his own image and his struggle to establish an identity in exile. The artist must have spent hours before a mirror, changing facial expressions and scrutinizing his features. His face is always rendered with great detail, whereas his torso is often only indicated by means of a few strokes. In this group of works, Nussbaum's power as a draftsman and his obsessive search for self-knowledge came together to produce some of the most compelling examples of his oeuvre.

Varying headgear play a part in Nussbaum's delineation of the different roles he assumed pictorially. Wearing a paper hat he contorts his face into a grimace (No. 39). Standing before a drawing board, his head wrapped in a cloth and his face full of questions, he pensively fingers his lower lip (No. 40). Elsewhere, wearing a beret, his frightened eyes and downturned mouth are framed in shadow (No. 41). At times Nussbaum hid his face from us and from himself entirely (No. 42). Around 1939, many of these drawings were incorporated into

36. *Self-Portrait with Dishtowel*, ca. 1935

Mummenschanz (No. 52), which represents the culmination of his grappling with the theme of exile as he experienced it in the 1930s, before the beginning of the War.

Mummenschanz owes a great deal to the art of James Ensor, both for its imagery and luminous color. Ensor's influence could already be seen around 1930, in the masked figure and skeletons of *Funeral* (No. 12). After moving to Ostend, Nussbaum sought out this city's most famous living artist. When Nussbaum wanted to renew his Belgian visa in September 1935, Ensor was one of two Ostend residents who wrote to the police on Nussbaum's behalf. The police dossier contains Ensor's remarks praising Nussbaum's art.[72]

Ostend was the site of an annual Carnival during which residents wearing masks and costumes cavorted in the streets. Ensor's mother ran a curio shop that sold Carnival masks, and the masks in his paintings derive from this Ostend tradition.[73] However, Ensor transformed the Carnival and its trappings into visions of horror. He used the masks to represent human falsehood and vice. As Libby Tannenbaum has noted: "There can be no question but that the carnival came to represent to Ensor the utter and abominable degradation of mankind."[74] The masked figures in a work like Ensor's *Masks Confronting Death* (see ill.) "are projections of Ensor's misanthropy and feelings of persecution"[75]; they threaten the artist. In Nussbaum's *Mummenschanz* all the masked figures are representations of the artist himself. Nussbaum borrowed Ensor's powerful imagery and inverted its meaning.

The two foreground figures in *Mummenschanz* are familiar to us from the series of self-portrait charcoal drawings of 1936 (Nos. 39 and 42), as is the figure in the left background with the beret (compare No. 41). The central figure with staring eyes and his hand raised to his mouth is a reworking of a gouache, *Self-Portrait in the Studio*, from around 1939 (No. 51).

In this gouache, the studio is bare except for a portfolio leaning against the wall and a framed blank canvas hanging above it. The perspective is distorted so that the space appears to be rushing toward the viewer instead of receding. It is the way rooms sometimes appear in dreams, where objects are laden with an unknown significance, and familiar things and spaces are distorted just enough to become terrifying. Nussbaum's torso looms in the foreground, wearing the artist's beret. With his hand raised to his mouth and his wide-eyed stare, he looks as though he had just experienced an awful vision.

The pose, gesture, and elements of dress have been carried over from *Self-Portrait in the Studio* to the central figure of *Mummenschanz*, but the additions of an earring and necklace introduce the notion of sexual ambiguity. Here the expression is more one of puzzled reflection than of horror.

The central figure in the background is also adapted

Opposite upper left:
52. *Mummenschanz (Masquerade)*, ca. 1939

Opposite left to right:
39. *Grimacing Self-Portrait with Paper Hat*, 1936

51. *Self-Portrait in the Studio*, ca. 1939

42. *Masked Self-Portrait with Paper Hat and Paper Horn*, ca. 1936

Right: James Ensor. *Masks Confronting Death*, 1888. Oil on canvas, 32 × 39½". The Museum of Modern Art, New York. Mrs. Simon Guggenheim Fund

45. *Man at the Window (Self-Portrait after Adriaen van Ostade)*, 1937

53. *European Vision*, 1939

from another self-portrait, *Man at the Window* of 1937 (No. 45). Nussbaum altered his features to resemble the type of figure found in the art of the seventeenth-century Netherlandish painter Adriaen van Ostade; the prominent nose and hands, and the gesture of hand to mouth are characteristic of Ostade, and the compositional device of a figure at a window parallel to the picture plane also occurs in Ostade.[76] Here Nussbaum represented himself as a tittering fool, withdrawn from reality into his own world of art. The broken pane of glass, however, indicates that the intrusion of the real world cannot be prevented.[77]

The last figure in *Mummenschanz* (right background) is not based on any single earlier work and is the most monstrous. We recognize the top hat from a number of other paintings (e.g. Nos. 12 and 14), where it has macabre connotations, and the bulging eye and top hat have precedents in Ensor.

In *Mummenschanz* Nussbaum gathered together the various aspects of his own personality that he had been exploring for several years and placed them on parade for his own scrutiny: the grimace of pain made ludicrous by the silly hat and earrings; the anonymous reveler; the serious, brooding artist; the withdrawn dreamer; the grotesque; and in the center — surrounded by all these other manifestations of the self — the androgynous questioner. Three other motifs from Nussbaum's earlier work

are also incorporated: the bare tree, the white sun from *Underpass in Rapallo* (No. 30), and the Berlin radio tower. The masquerade takes place in an unidentified space, a barren, eerie landscape on the left, the congestion and anonymity of a big city on the right. Both environments are threatening and inhospitable. This is Nussbaum's vision of life as an exile: uncertain identity and the alienation from one's fellow men and from one's surroundings.

During the years 1938 and 1939 conditions in Nazi Germany became increasingly dangerous for Jews. On the night of November 9–10, 1938, anti-Jewish pogroms took place throughout Germany: synagogues were destroyed, Jewish businesses looted, and male Jews were sent to concentration camps (see Nos. 106 and 107). Many Jews who had heretofore been reluctant to leave Germany now felt the necessity to emigrate; but by late 1938 it was difficult to find countries that would accept them. With the declaration of war on September 1, 1939, legal emigration became virtually impossible.

This changing political climate is reflected in Nussbaum's art. *European Vision* of 1939 (No. 53) expresses the plight of the persecuted seeking refuge. A man sits despondently with his head in his hands. The bundle and walking stick by his side identify him as a homeless wanderer. The room in which he sits is dominated by a globe, turned so that the map of Europe faces the

44. *Self-Portrait with Brother*, 1937

49. *Self-Portrait in a Surreal Landscape,*
ca. 1939

viewer. The table's distorted perspective creates a space suffused with anxiety. The wanderer's distance from the globe and his dispairing posture suggest he will not find a safe haven. Through an arched opening one sees a barren landscape with leafless trees, representing a hostile and inhospitable world.

Four works from around 1939 represent figures in unstable surroundings.[78] Tottering buildings and slanting walls in environments of shifting and overlapping planes convey Nussbaum's perception of a world gone awry. In *Couple in a Surreal Landscape* (No. 50) we can assume that the man and woman stand for Felix and Felka. *Self-Portrait in a Surreal Landscape* (No. 49) depicts Nussbaum's troubled, oversized face superimposed on a scene that includes the image of the Berlin radio tower (compare No. 8). Nussbaum here acknowledged the demise of the metropolis he had known and loved as a young artist. Berlin, where he had developed his talent and enjoyed his only major public success, had become the city where, on March 20, 1939, 4,829 works by so-

50. *Couple in a Surreal Landscape*, ca. 1939

called "degenerate artists" were consigned to the flames.

The years of exile had taken a tremendous toll on Nussbaum's relationship with Felka Platek. On October 6, 1937, they had married, hoping that this act of acquiescence to the demands of middle-class society would finally obtain for them the desired "yellow card," a two-year residence permit. Despite their marriage they were only granted another six-month renewal.

It has been suggested that *Self-Portrait with Brother* of 1937 (No. 44) may well reflect Nussbaum's feelings that his marriage signified his conforming to middle-class standards. To Felix, the artist and self-styled Bohemian, his older brother Justus represented respectability and bourgeois societal norms. Justus had gone into the family business, married, established a family. He was the practical son while Felix was the dreamer. In the painting Justus represents reality while Felix, with his painted face and pointed hat, resembles a clown, trying to keep reality at bay. Their father, who had always validated Felix as an artist and supported him in the

fraternal conflict, cannot help him now; he is the man with the walking stick leaving the scene.[79] Felix's collar and pointed hat and the white makeup on his face relate to the left foreground figure in *Mummenschanz* (No. 52), but here the grimace has been replaced by a look of withdrawn resignation.

Without a knowledge of the biographical details one can still understand this painting as a study of contrasting personality types: the inward, somewhat melancholy Felix and his laughing, outgoing brother Justus.[80] The expressions of the two brothers in this painting bear an uncanny resemblance to their appearances in a photograph taken around 1928 during a New Year's Eve party (No. 96, ill. p. 85). In this photograph Felix appears lost in thought, whereas the camera caught Justus in the middle of a hearty laugh, his mouth wide open. The conception of this painting is similar to Hans von Marées' famous self-portrait with his friend the painter Franz von Lenbach.[81] In both works a somber foreground figure with a large dark hat (Lenbach and Felix

47. *Still Life with Barred Window*, 1938

Nussbaum) partially obscures the more animated face of the second figure (Marées and Justus Nussbaum).

Nussbaum's sense of entrapment in his marriage found expression in a number of works.[82] Indications of tension between Felix and Felka are already present in a portrait of her executed around 1936 (No. 43), part of the series of large-format charcoal drawings (Nos. 39–43). There is a total absence of tenderness in this portrait. Nussbaum depicts Felka with hard features and a pinched mouth. He does, however, acknowledge her as an artist, by portraying her in a smock, and there are signs of a grudging respect in the solidity with which he endows her imposing figure.[83]

The sense of being trapped is strongly conveyed in *Still Life with Barred Window* of 1938 (No. 47), where the viewer is directly confronted by a vase containing paintbrushes and a flower with a broken stem. The vase is hemmed in by a masonry wall at back and another wall pierced by a barred window at right. The brushes must in some way represent Nussbaum himself. Similarly, the flower may be a visual metaphor for his relationship with Felka. A long tradition of still-life painting employed wilted or dying flowers to symbolize transience. Here the flower may represent the fragility of the couple's love and the decay of their marriage. Owing to the difficult circumstances of exile, Felix and Felka could not separate; they needed to stay together in order to survive. In *Still Life with Barred Window* Nussbaum expressed his sense of being imprisoned by his marriage and by the political forces that had forced him into this situation. The significance of this image is indicated by the fact that he painted it twice.[84]

Further evidence of Felix's estrangement from Felka is provided by *Self-Portrait with an Appleblossom* of 1939 (No. 48). Nussbaum appears in the foreground behind a leafless tree, situated in a desolate landscape with a wall, truncated trees, and birds in a dark sky. The shadowy figure of a woman emerges in the background by the wall. She and Nussbaum are separated by a patch of darkness, a seemingly unbreachable gulf.[85] The flowers in the woman's hands and the single appleblossom between his lips allude to a former happier time.

The tension between Felix and Felka was intensified by events that took place in the late spring of 1939. Philipp and Rahel Nussbaum finally decided to leave Germany and wanted to join Felix in Brussels. Felka could only have been dismayed at the prospect of her in-laws coming to live with them in their small two-room apartment at 22 Rue Archimède. Felix's close relationship with his father, the parents' disapproval of Felka, and the problems that already existed between the couple, must have sent Felka into a panic at the thought

43. *Portrait of Felka Platek*, ca. 1936

60. *Portrait of Felka Platek*, 1940

54. *The Secret (1)*, 1939

55. *The Secret (2)*, November 1939

58. *Studio in Brussels*, 1940

59. *Still Life with Lay Figure*, ca. 1940

of the elder Nussbaums' moving in with them. She sent anonymous letters to the authorities, which thwarted the Nussbaums' immigration to Belgium.[86] Instead, they went to Amsterdam to join their elder son, Justus, who had succeeded in reestablishing himself in business since his immigration in 1937.

Nussbaum's awareness of this betrayal and his reaction to the outbreak of war in September 1939 are contained in one of his strongest paintings, *The Secret*, dated November 1939 (No. 55). Here, the viewer experiences the anxiety and foreboding created by the whispered secret and the rooms that open onto one another into oblivion. The terrifying unknown at left is balanced by the symbol of domestic security, the dishtowel, at right. Between these elements, three figures, each bearing some resemblance to the artist, whisper, listen, and indicate silence. The gestures associated with these activities are emphasized by the large size of the hands in proportion to the size of the bodies of the figures, as well as by the central position of the hands, which form a triangle within the larger triangle created by the trio of figures. Nussbaum's development of this pyramidlike composition may be studied in the sketch he did in the margin of the preparatory drawing for *The Secret* (No. 54). The drawing also reveals Nussbaum's interest in the interrelationship between the two checkered patterns, straight in the floor tiles and billowing in the dishtowel.

The effect of these secrets—her betrayal and the onslaught of the Nazi armies in Europe—on Felka, and the further deterioration of the Nussbaums' marriage is made painfully clear in the 1940 portrait of Felka (No. 60). With tightly pursed lips and empty stare, her arms clenched around her, she appears frightened and lonely. We need only compare this with the 1936 portrait (No. 43) to see how greatly she has been changed by events.

As the net seemed to close tighter around them, Nussbaum began to paint more still lifes, views of the rooms in which he lived, and what could be seen from his window, a practice that would continue during the years in hiding. A gouache of 1940, *Studio in Brussels* (No. 58), documents Nussbaum's workspace and includes some of the objects that show up in his still-life compositions. For example, the articulated mannequin on the table appears in *Still Life with Lay Figure* (No. 59). Like *The Secret*, this still life demonstrates a new interest in compositions built of geometric forms: cylinder, square, and triangle. Nussbaum's use of the draftsman's triangle may be inspired by De Chirico and other Italian artists of the *Pittura Metafisica* style, such as Carlo Carrà and Mario Sironi.[87] The triangle, on the one hand, represents a return to order, after the shifting planes of Nussbaum's surreal landscape series (Nos. 49 and 50). On the other hand, we are reminded of De Chirico's statement:

56. *View of Rooftops in Brussels (Gloves)*, 1940

Giorgio de Chirico. *The Song of Love*, 1914. Oil on canvas, 28³⁄₄ × 23³⁄₈″. The Museum of Modern Art, New York.

Often in the past geometrical figures have been interpreted as portentous symbols of a higher reality. In antiquity, for instance, and now in theosophic doctrine, the triangle is considered a mystic and magic symbol, and beyond question, it arouses in the beholder, even when he is ignorant of its significance, a feeling of apprehension, perhaps even of fear.[88]

The cause of this fear is hinted at in Nussbaum's still life by the presence of the newspaper, referring to the terrible political realities of the day.[89]

During this period a motif appears that seems to have had particular significance for Nussbaum: the glove.[90] In *View of Rooftops in Brussels (Gloves)* of 1940 (No. 56) the artist painted an ordinary urban view from his studio window, with a startling addition: two huge gloves on a line, hanging by clothespins.

The glove as fetish in art was first presented in the remarkable series of prints by Max Klinger, entitled *A Glove* (first edition, 1881). In Klinger's etchings the glove is the object of sexual obsession, a form simultaneously phallic and yonic.[91] Klinger's series greatly impressed De Chirico, who incorporated a glove into a number of compositions, among them *The Song of Love* of 1914 (see ill.), which was probably the source for Nussbaum's imagery.[92] The contrasts in scale and the unexpected conjunction of the object with its environ-

ment derive from De Chirico. Painted in Paris, *The Song of Love* remained there for some time and had great influence on artists in France and Belgium.[93] A glove appears in a still life by Nussbaum from about 1940 (No. 57), juxtaposed with a ball, a reference, perhaps, to De Chirico's *The Song of Love*.

Like the dishtowel,[94] the glove was a private symbol, the exact meaning of which cannot be determined. Gloves cover and protect the hand; they may also conceal it. The hand, of course, is one of the primary tools of the painter. That the meaning of the glove is bound up with Nussbaum's *métier* is suggested by the self-portrait with mask and palette (No. 33), where the painter holds up a gloved hand. The glove constricts the hand's movement and also keeps it from being soiled with paint. The analogy, in this particular self-portrait, between the mask concealing the painter's face, and the glove that sheathes his hand, also bears considering. The glove offers multiple associations for Nussbaum, obsessed as he was with his identity as an artist and his powerlessness as a pawn in history. It has also been suggested that the glove relates to Nussbaum's being forbidden to undertake employment under the terms of his residence permit (see No. 105), and his need to affirm that his work as an artist was valuable, and qualified as "real" work.[95]

73. *Prisoners at St. Cyprien (3),* 1942

ST. CYPRIEN: 1940

Whatever intimations of doom Nussbaum had had while in Ostend and Brussels must have paled in comparison to the reality of the conditions he experienced in the internment camp of St. Cyprien. (See Sybil Milton's essay page 70ff.) The horrors of the prisoners' lives there are recorded in a number of drawings Nussbaum made during his internment. Once he had escaped and returned to Brussels where he went underground, he translated these drawings into two oil paintings, *The Camp Synagogue* of 1941 (No. 65) and *Prisoners at St. Cyprien* of 1942 (No. 73).

Prisoners at St. Cyprien was developed through a number of highly detailed drawings (Nos. 61–63) depicting refugees huddled around a makeshift table on which stands a globe. The abstract fear expressed in *European Vision* (No. 53) has become a palpable reality. St. Cyprien was an environment of sand and barbed wire, and these elements dominate Nussbaum's renditions. The discarded boots refer to the pair of shoes each prisoner wore at the time of arrest, and which fell apart in a matter of weeks.[96]

Figures from Nussbaum's past and future works are gathered around the globe, which offers no country of refuge. The man to the right of the globe with furrowed brow and blue eyes wide with terror, was the "listener" in *The Secret* (No. 55); here his neat shirt and bow tie have been replaced by rags. Behind him, to the left, is a nude with shaven head who resembles many of the figures Nussbaum would paint in hiding (see Nos. 71 and 84). Nussbaum himself appears with a bindlestiff over his shoulder, a reference both to the wanderer in *European Vision,* and to his plans for escape.

Nussbaum's intention to survive St. Cyprien and record his experiences in paint is attested to by the inscription on one of the drawings (No. 63, ill. p. 71), which reads (in German): "study for a painting." This drawing reveals all the artist's skill and delicacy as a draftsman. His responsiveness to texture and his special love for the patterns found in woodgraining come to the fore in this work, and his interest in linear design created an ironically beautiful web out of the barbed wire.

Nussbaum did not have this drawing with him when he painted the oil in 1942; he had given it to a fellow prisoner, most likely because this man had a visa and was leaving the camp,[97] and the artist saw this as an opportunity to preserve his work. There are minor differences between the drawing (No. 63) and the painting (No. 73). In the painting, a mandolin replaced the violin, and

Nussbaum added a rat, barbed wire, and an empty can to the foreground. The most significant change occurs in the globe itself. In the drawing it resembles a real globe, except that neither land nor water is indicated: the world is still intact, though it offers little hope of refuge for the prisoners. In the painting the globe is made of papier-mâché held together with barbed wire; by June of 1942 the world seemed to Nussbaum to have fallen apart, held together only by the symbol of Nazi terror and domination.

The musical instruments in *Prisoners at St. Cyprien* refer to the cultural life that inmates created, despite the harsh conditions. The violin is a poignant echo of the music implied in *The Classical Singing Lesson* of 1935 (No. 32).

The second major work to emerge from St. Cyprien, *The Camp Synagogue* (see Nos. 64 and 65) is completely different in mood. Instead of the dismal beige and browns of sand and tattered clothing and the sharp green behind the barbed wire in *Prisoners at St. Cyprien, The Camp Synagogue* is built of subtly modulated tones of rich brown and an incandescent violet. The somber areas are punctuated by the figures wrapped in white prayer shawls. All the men have their backs to us and to those objects in the foreground that represent the harsh reality of camp life: barbed wire, a bone, an empty tin can, and a worn-out shoe. Cocooned in their prayer shawls, they have withdrawn into religion that seems to provide a respite from the horrors of camp life.[98] Four figures pray together, a fifth stands apart. It is tempting to see the

fifth figure as the artist, wrapping himself in the symbol of his heritage as he did in *The Two Jews* of 1926 (No. 3). *The Camp Synagogue* marks Nussbaum's return to Jewish subject matter.

BRUSSELS: LIFE IN HIDING 1940–44

The works produced in hiding chronicle Nussbaum's struggle to survive, his feelings of persecution, and the fear that was his constant companion. As the years progressed, the color was drained from his work, until— with a few notable exceptions—his paintings were dominated by browns, beiges, grays, and olive-green.

Fear of 1941 (No. 66), depicts Nussbaum with Justus's daughter, Marianne. Tacked to a wall behind them is a paper with the words "Tempête sur l'Europe" (storm over Europe) and "PÉRIL AÉRIENNE" (aerial peril), references to the war and the German bombing missions. The inclusion of his niece points to the common fate of the Nussbaum family; whether in Brussels or Amsterdam they are terrified, seeking refuge from the Nazi "storm over Europe."

Images of anguish, like the *Weeping Woman* (No. 68) with her barbed-wire choker, abound in the works of 1941. *Despairing Women* (No. 67) repeats the motifs of wall and trees with lopped-off branches. Here the anthropomorphic quality of Nussbaum's trees, the branches of which often appear like fingers clawing at the sky, is explicitly stated: the form of the raised arm of the

56

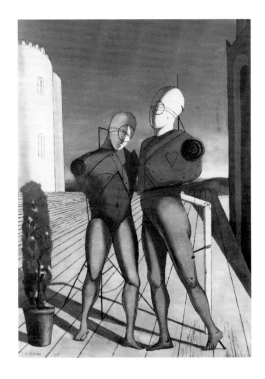

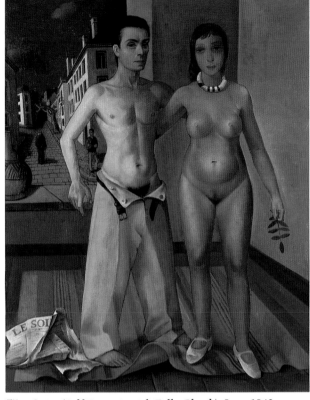

75. *Soir (Self-Portrait with Felka Platek),* June 1942

78. *Mannequins,* 1943

woman at right is echoed by the bent branch of the tree behind her.

In *Loneliness* of 1942 (No. 71), the trees have grown to terrifying heights; the clouds float at a level only halfway up the trunks. Walls of wooden planks seem about to collapse under the weight of the trees. Caught between the narrow passageway created by the walls and trees are two androgynous figures: a lifesize mannequin holding a megaphone — an allusion perhaps to the masquerade (compare Nos. 42 and 52) — and the nude from *Prisoners at St. Cyprien* (Nos. 62, 63, and 73).

In January 1942 Felix and Felka Nussbaum fled their apartment because it had become known to the Gestapo, and were taken in by the sculptor Dolf Ledel and his family. When the Ledels left Brussels, probably around June 1942, the Nussbaums returned to 22 Rue Archimède, but not to their former apartment; instead they moved into the attic. Their situation at this critical juncture is reflected in *Soir (Self–Portrait with Felka Platek)* of June 1942 (No. 75).

Felix and Felka stand in an interior, empty except for a small rug and the newspaper *Le Soir.* This paper, which gave them the daily news, also published the orders of the German military occupation forces. (For example, the order for Jews to wear the yellow star, see No. 113.) An opening in the back wall provides a view of Rue Archimède beneath a gray sky: the couple are standing in a place of peril, their apartment that had become known to the authorities. The newspaper represents current political events and provides the impetus

71. *Loneliness*, 1942

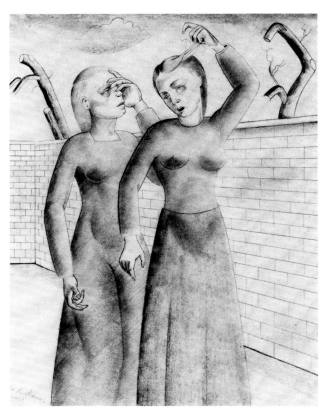

67. *Despairing Women*, 1941

68. *Weeping Woman*, 1941

for flight, but Felix and Felka are unable to flee. He is partially dressed, but barefoot; she wears shoes, but is otherwise unclad. Signs of attempted movement are found in the rumpled carpet, possibly indicating that Felka thwarted Felix's attempt to escape, since her foot seems to be stepping on his.

The Nussbaums' estranged marital situation is expressed in their stiff locked embrace, which maintains distance despite their linked arms. They are bound together by circumstances and no longer by choice. Their nudity may be an ironic reference to Adam and Eve.

The woman bears little actual resemblance to Felka (compare Nos. 43 and 60). Her full breasts and rounded belly suggest an idealized image of womanhood. Felka's appearance is similar to that of Paula Modersohn-Becker, as seen in her self-portraits. The large dark eyes, flat handling of the facial features, choker of large beads, and the camelia twig held in her hand are remarkably close to Modersohn-Becker's *Self-Portrait with Camelia Branch* of 1907.[99]

With its juxtaposition of interior and exterior space, *Soir* expresses thoughts of escape, and the inability to realize these plans. *Mannequins* of 1943 (No. 78), reinterprets the forms of the figures in *Soir* and removes them from any realistic context. The lay figures from

Nussbaum's studio (see Nos. 58 and 59) have been transformed into lifesize projections of the artist and his wife. The stance of the mannequins, their linked arms, so similar to that of the Nussbaums in *Soir*, establishes this identification. Nussbaum's *Mannequins* is clearly dependent on the *manichino* of Giorgio de Chirico; particularly those in the more sentimental paintings by the Italian master that feature a pair of mannequins, for example *The Duo* of 1915 (see ill.). In many of De Chirico's *manichino* paintings the ground is covered with wooden planking that stretches out under an open sky, creating a sense of uncertainty as to whether the scene takes place indoors or out. Nussbaum appropriated De Chirico's dramatically raked floorboards, which here rise steeply from the foreground. Nussbaum's appreciation for the patterns of woodgraining no doubt made these floorboards and wooden lay figures especially attractive to him as subjects. The ambiguity of indoor and outdoor space was particularly relevant to the theme of life in hiding.

The *manichino* was De Chirico's most influential iconographic theme, and was reinterpreted by artists such as Carlo Carrà, Mario Sironi, Max Ernst, George Grosz, and Oskar Schlemmer.[100] Many of these artists used this motif to address the issue of mechanization in society and the anonymity of modern man, endowing the man-

83. *Still Life with Doll and Tennis Racquet,* June 1943

85. *Self-Portrait at the Easel*, August 1943

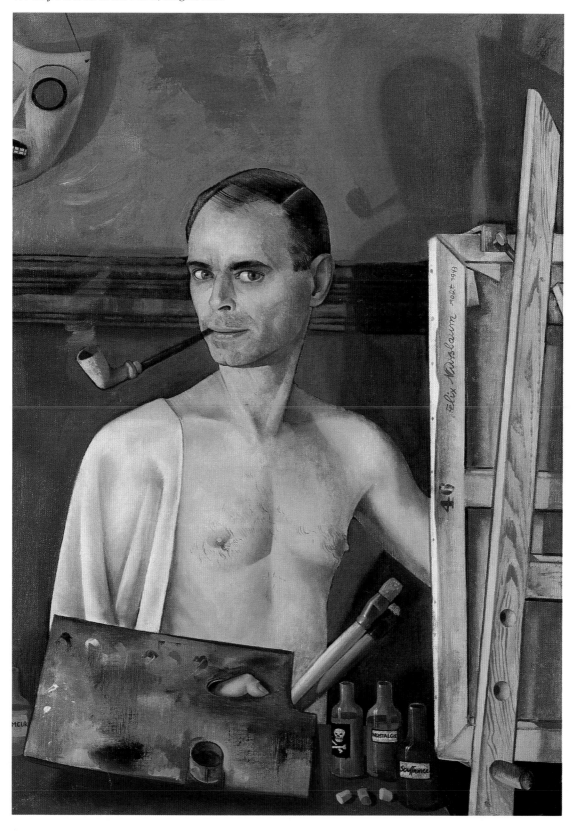

82. *Still Life with Egg*, March 1943

nequin with negative connotations. This was a departure from De Chirico, who saw the mannequin as a symbol of the poet, as a figure of self-identification for the artist.[101] Nussbaum returned to De Chirico's original conception of the mannequin, treating it as a projection of himself and Felka.

Blind and mute, the mannequins are expressive metaphors for the Nussbaums' role as pawns in political circumstances over which they have no control. The mannequins are figures of tremendous pathos, powerless yet dignified. In the left background of *Mannequins* another lifesize lay figure peers through a telescope, as if trying to see into the future to determine the fate of these jointed puppets.

Turned in upon himself and the narrow confines of his attic and cellar dwellings, Nussbaum executed a number of still lifes in 1943, some of which bear exact dates; they constitute a kind of diary of life in hiding. Some, like *The Kitchen in Hiding* (No. 79), are detailed and straightforward depictions of his surroundings. Others (see Nos. 81 and 82) are arrangements of simple household objects, with a static grandeur reminiscent of works by Giorgio Morandi.

Still Life with Doll and Tennis Racquet (No. 83) depicts a number of seemingly unrelated objects to

which Nussbaum had access while in hiding: the doll and tennis racquet belonged to members of the Billestraet family, in whose basement on the Rue General Gratry the Nussbaums had their second secret dwelling; the dishtowel is a familiar Nussbaum motif; and the vase is the type of painted ceramic that Nussbaum produced and sold in order to support himself and Felka (see Nos. 76 and 77). The doll, ball, and racquet are all objects associated with play, leisure, and a carefree existence, the towel represents domestic security, and the images on the vase relate to Nussbaum's past and memories of a happier world: the windmill of his youth (see No. 5), the wheel of Osnabrück, the sunflower that appeared in different guises in his art (see Nos. 13, 16, and 32), and the cart and blue skies of Italy (see Nos. 20 and 23).[102] Thus, the objects collected for this still life express a yearning for a normal and pleasurable life such as Nussbaum experienced prior to 1933. The juxtaposition of the doll, ball, and tennis racquet also has resonances of Carlo Carrà's paintings of mannequins, tennis racquets, and balls,[103] and Anton Räderscheidt's images of female tennis players.[104]

In 1943 Nussbaum painted three important canvases that offered different aspects of his state of mind during that year. *Self-Portrait at the Easel* (No. 85) is an effort to keep fear at bay by resorting to irony; it also reaffirmed his commitment to art and his identity as an artist. Fixing the viewer with a steady gaze, a pipe held jauntily between his lips, he fashions his art using the substances from bottles labeled *humeur* (humor), *nostalgie* (nostalgia), and *souffrance* (suffering). A fourth bottle is marked only by a skull and crossbones. Nussbaum depicts himself unclothed; there is nothing to indicate his poverty or political status, no shabby coat or Jewish star. He presents himself in his essence — as an artist.

In *Organ Grinder* (No. 84), begun in June 1942 and only finished the following July, the protagonist looks out of the picture, turning his back on the carnage in the street. The sense of foreboding in the long street hung with banners depicted in *Fishwife in Harbor* (No. 38) has been fully realized in this scene of destruction. Even the pipes of the hurdy-gurdy are made of bones. The organ grinder seems impervious to these grisly elements, so lost is he in his own thoughts; Nussbaum's alter ego, the organ grinder, is resigned to his fate.

The third painting in this group, *Self-Portrait with Jewish Identity Card* (No. 86), has previously been discussed as an image both of terror and the acceptance of the artist's status as a Jew and a man without a country. Together these three canvases present three modes of response to Nussbaum's situation: bravado and the bolstering of self-confidence through identification as

84. *Organ Grinder,* July 1943

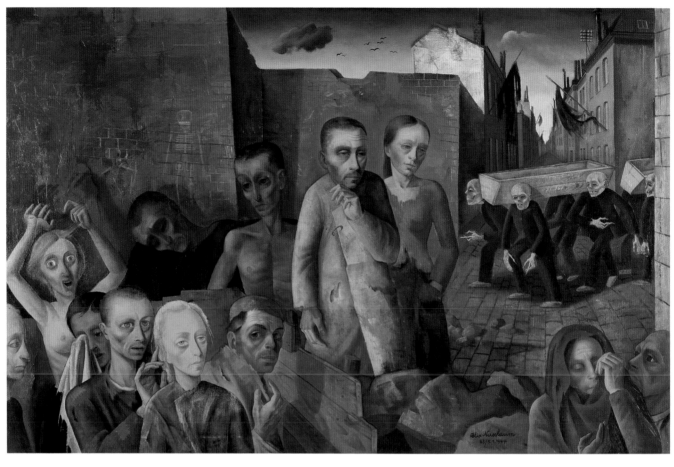

89. *The Damned (2)*, 1943/5 January 1944

88. *The Damned (1)*, ca. 1943

an artist; withdrawn resignation; and panic coupled with the acceptance of his identity as a Jew.

This acceptance of Jewish identity precipitated a number of emotion-filled paintings expressing the plight of Jews in Nazi-occupied Europe; for example, *Grieving Couple* (No. 87) and *Jacqui on the Street* (No. 90). Jacqui — a young boy who often shared Nussbaum's hiding place on Rue General Gratry — is depicted as alone, lost, helpless, and exposed, his yellow star prominent on his coat. It is the archetypal image of the isolated Jew, abandoned by the world.

Nussbaum brought the figures from many of these paintings together in *The Damned* (Nos. 88 and 89). The preparatory drawing (No. 88) depicts four people on the landing of a staircase: the man at right in this group is a reworking of *Self-Portrait with Jewish Identity Card* (No. 86), the woman next to him closely resembles Felka as she appears in the portrait of 1940 (No. 60). Two additional figures with stars on their coats stand in the center. Rubble and boulders are everywhere. Receding into the background at right is the long street decked with dark flags, which we recognize from other works. In the left background there are more ruins and the Cross of Golgotha. We are witnessing the aftermath of destruction. The people in the foreground are the survivors.

A notation in the right margin of the drawing calls for "Gaslampe" (gas lamp) and "Gerippe" (skeletons). In the final painted version, dated 1943/5 January 1944 (No. 89), the skeletons appear from the right carrying coffins. The conception of the painting is drastically altered from that of the drawing: instead of depicting survivors, the painting truly depicts the damned. A high wall bearing pictures of skeletons replaces the rubble in the drawing, and there is no view into the distance at left (compare *Funeral*, No. 12.). Felix and Felka are joined by ten people whose faces are marked with varying expressions of fear, horror, despondency, or blank resignation; figures we recognize from earlier works, such as *Weeping Woman* (No. 68) and *Organ Grinder* (No. 84). They seem to be awaiting transport to death.[105] The skeletons carry coffins bearing the numbers 25367 and 25368 — Nussbaum could hardly have known that is this roughly the number of Jews deported from Belgium to their deaths.[106]

The tremendous shift in meaning that occurred between the first and second version may have been due to Nussbaum's knowledge that his family in Amsterdam had been deported to the Westerbork camp in August 1943. By this time news of the Nazi death camps had reached the Allies, and Nussbaum's friends kept him informed of news they heard on the Allied radio broadcasts. Today we know that the reality of these camps was

90. *Jaqui on the Street*, late January 1944

far worse than even Nussbaum imagined.

Nussbaum's last extant work, *The Skeletons Play for a Dance* (No. 93), is dated 18 April 1944. A compositional sketch (No. 91) and a detailed study of three skeletons playing musical instruments (No. 92) also survive.

The concept of the painting derives from the iconographic tradition of the *Totentanz* (Dance of Death), which dates from medieval times.[107] Music-making skeletons play and dance amid the ruins of Western civilization. The foreground is littered with objects representing the sciences, technology, the arts, and daily life. Private symbols — Felix's father's car, Felka's dressmaker's dummy, and Jacqui's bicycle — are also included.

At first glance, the work seems like yet another terrifying vision of destruction. Closer analysis reveals many positive elements. The wall that had formerly blocked Nussbaum's path since the paintings of the early 1930s has finally been torn down, the fearsome trees appear broken, the threatening clouds are being blown away, and the birds of prey have disappeared. Airplanes in the sky represent the Allied bombers that have finally vanquished the enemy.[108]

All the figures are skeletons, with the exception of the organ grinder. He is painfully thin, but alive, and we can recognize Nussbaum's features in his gaunt face. The subject of the painting is the world after the defeat of the Nazi forces. Much has been destroyed, but Nussbaum counted himself among the survivors. By April 1944 news of the Allied advances must have made liberation seem imminent. Nussbaum thought he had pulled through.

In July 1944 the Gestapo discovered Felix and Felka Nussbaum in the attic of 22 Rue Archimède and sent them to the transit camp of Malines (see No. 118). They were in the last group deported from Malines to Auschwitz, on July 31. Upon their arrival there on August 3, 1944, just one month before the liberation of Brussels, Felix and Felka Nussbaum were murdered.

Nussbaum's search for a place of physical safety proved unsuccessful, but he did find a kind of refuge in his art. His art was a haven, "like the shade of a massive rock in a languishing land."[109] It was one of the means by which he retained his spirit throughout the ordeal of exile, internment, and hiding. Despite the risks involved, he had his paintings brought to the studio of the photographer Robert Martin between 1942 and 1944 to insure that a record of his work would survive even if he did not. Sometime after June 1942 he brought paintings to Dr. Josef Grosfils for safekeeping, telling him: "If I perish, do not let my pictures die; show them to the public." Nussbaum's artistic legacy affords us insights into the experiences of one man, and through him, of the generation which shared his fate. Above all, it confirms the ability of creativity and the human spirit to triumph over adversity.

NOTES

All translations, unless otherwise indicated, are by the author.

1. *Widerstand statt Anpassung. Deutsche Kunst im Widerstand gegen den Faschismus 1933–1945*, ed. Badischer Kunstverein, Karlsruhe and Elefanten Press (Berlin, 1980).
2. Janet Blatter and Sybil Milton, *Art of the Holocaust* (New York, 1981).
3. H. J. Müller in *Die Zeit*, no. 7, February 8, 1980, 27.
4. Peter Junk and Wendelin Zimmer, *Felix Nussbaum: Leben und Werk* (Cologne and Bramsche, 1982), 251. Compare the tree and courtyard depicted in Nussbaum's drawing of March 5, 1942, inscribed with this Brussels address, No. 72 in this exhibition.
5. *Ibid.*, 191.
6. Kulturgeschichtliches Museum, Osnabrück, *Informationsblätter und Postkarten zur Dauerausstellung Felix Nussbaum und die Zeit 1904–1944*, ed. Eva Berger, Peter Junk, Karl Georg Kaster, and Wendelin Zimmer (Bramsche, 1983/4), flyer no. 2, "Felix Nussbaum, *Landstrasse mit malendem Felix Nussbaum, 1928*," 1.
7. See, for example, Philipp Nussbaum's painting from the 1920s, *Sandkuhle in der Barlage*, ill. in Junk and Zimmer, *Nussbaum*, 21.
8. Margarete Hellman, Osnabrück, February 25, 1971. See *ibid.*, 20.
9. *Ibid.*, 22.
10. *Ibid.*, 22.
11. See chronology in this catalogue, pp. 82–87.
12. This represents an interesting departure from the work of E. M. Lilien, whose illustrations for *Die Bücher der Bibel* (Berlin/Vienna, 1908) were probably a source for Nussbaum. Compare, for example, the flat silhouette of the man in Nussbaum's drawing with the figure in Lilien's illustration with which it is compared in Junk and Zimmer, *Nussbaum*, ill., 28.
13. Nussbaum seems to have modeled the portrait of his grandparents' housekeeper, Talea, on Van Gogh's series of portraits of Mme. Augustine Roulin. See J.-B. de la Faille, *The Works of Vincent van Gogh. His Paintings and Drawings* (rev. ed.; Amsterdam, 1970), nos. F 504–08. Nussbaum adopted a similar pose for his figure and incorporated the swirling patterns of Van Gogh's backgrounds, albeit somewhat tamed, into Talea's dress.
14. Compare Van Gogh's numerous paintings of sunflowers, De la Faille nos. F 454–58. Sunflowers apparently had a symbolic significance for Nussbaum vis-à-vis his mother. A double-sided canvas bears a portrait of his mother on one side and a vase of sunflowers, dated 1928, on the other, (Junk and Zimmer, *Nussbaum*, nos. 44 and 43). Probably the most blatant instances of Nussbaum's emulation of Van Gogh occurred in *Erinnerung an Grussau*, 1925 (*ibid.*, no. 2) and during a trip to the south of France in 1929, when Nussbaum painted a view of Les Alycamps in Arles (*ibid.*, no. 53). Compare Van Gogh's versions of this motif, De la Faille nos. F 486–87, 568–69. For Nussbaum's admiration of Van Gogh, see also the memoirs of Hermann Wilhelm, a fellow student of Paul Plontke in Berlin, *Erinnerungen I, 1900–1931* (Nuremberg, n.d.), 96. I would like to thank Karl Georg Kaster for providing me with the relevant pages from Wilhelm's memoirs.
15. See Osnabrück, flyer no. 3, "Felix Nussbaum, *Die beiden Juden*, 1926," 5.

93. *The Skeletons Play for a Dance*, 18 April 1944

92. *Skeletons Playing Musical Instruments* (preparatory
drawing for *The Skeletons Play for a Dance*), ca. 1944

16. The structure of the composition, with its symmetry of background elements, centrally positioned ark, and dislocation of foreground and background, are reminiscent of *Remain Pious*, No. 1 in this exhibition.

17. Letter of 1974, reprinted in Junk and Zimmer, *Nussbaum*, 30.

18. Osnabrück, flyer no. 3, 4.

19. See, for example, Junk and Zimmer, *Nussbaum*, 29.

20. Oppenheim, a successful portraitist and genre painter, created many works depicting traditional Jewish practices in home and synagogue. See, The Jewish Museum, *A Tale of Two Cities: Jewish Life in Frankfurt and Istanbul 1650–1870* (New York, 1982), nos. 99, 100, 102, 105, and 130; and The Israel Museum, *Moritz Oppenheim. The First Jewish Painter* (Jerusalem, 1983).

21. Alfred Werner, "Jewish Artists of the Age of Emancipation," in Cecil Roth, ed., *Jewish Art. An Illustrated History*, rev. ed. by Bezalel Narkiss (Greenwich, Connecticut, 1971), 199. For Gottlieb's painting, see fig. 225.

22. A painting of 1931, *Maler im Atelier* (*Painter in the Studio*; Junk and Zimmer, *Nussbaum*, no. 75), depicts Nussbaum interrupted in the act of painting a nude couple by the appearance of four men in long robes, who probably represent figures of traditional Judaism. See discussion and ill., *ibid.*, 32–34.

23. For more on Nussbaum's student years in Berlin, see *ibid.*, 38–50.

24. Paul Westheim in *Das Kunstblatt*, 11 (1927), no. 8, 318.

25. Willi Wolfradt, "Junge Deutsche Kunst. IX. Felix Nussbaum," *Die Horen*, 5 (1928/9), no. 9, 790.

26. See also *Mühle in Xanten*, 1927, Junk and Zimmer, *Nussbaum*, no. 18.

27. See, for example, Nos. 49 and 86 in this exhibition; and *ibid.*, nos. 37, 96, 124, 220, and 223.

28. *Am Funkturm*. See Wieland Schmied, *Neue Sachlichkeit und Magischer Realismus in Deutschland 1918–1933* (Hannover, 1969), 311, fig. 281.

29. Rousseau's particular brand of realism — the static dignity of objects suffused with a dream-like mystery — had a tremendous influence on German painters in their renunciation of the frenzy and dissolution of Expressionism. See Franz Roh, "Ein neuer Henri Rousseau," *Jahrbuch der jungen Kunst*, 1924, 57–59; Werner Haftmann, *Painting in the Twentieth Century*, I, trans. by Ralph Mannheim (New York, 1960), 168; and Wieland Schmied, "Die Neue Wirklichkeit — Surrealismus und Sachlichkeit," in Berlin, Neuer Nationalgalerie, *Tendenzen der Zwanziger Jahre*, 1977, 4/5–7.

30. See Osnabrück, flyer no. 2.

31. *Ibid.*, 4.

32. For De Chirico's influence in Germany see Wieland Schmied, "De Chirico and the Realism of the Twenties," in The Museum of Modern Art, *Giorgio de Chirico*, ed. William Rubin (New York, 1982), 101–09. The art and theories of *Pittura Metafisica* were disseminated by means of the periodical *Valori Plastici*, which published five issues between 1918 and 1921. In addition, its editor, Mario Broglio, issued books on a number of the movement's artists, including De Chirico, and organized two exhibitions of their work for circulation in Germany in 1921 and 1924. (I am indebted to Emily Braun for this information.) Shortly before Nussbaum painted *Memory of Norderney* in 1929, the Galerie Cassirer in Berlin had exhibited works by De Chirico, as had Galerie Flechtheim in 1928.

33. See James Thrall Soby, *Giorgio de Chirico* (New York, 1955), 98 and 106; and Schmied, *Tendenzen*, 4/4.

34. Osnabrück, flyer no. 4, "Felix Nussbaum, *Erinnerung an Norderney, 1929*," 3.

35. See *ibid.*, 4–5.

36. The elder Nussbaums' disapproval of their son's girlfriend may have been an example of the prejudice with which many German Jews regarded their coreligionists from eastern Europe.

37. Osnabrück, flyer no. 4, 5.

38. For paintings of Ostend from that student trip, see Junk and Zimmer, *Nussbaum*, nos. 38, 40, 41, and 48.

39. Quoted in Osnabrück, flyer no. 1, "Die künstlerischen Sehbedingungen des jungen Nussbaum," 2.

40. See also Junk and Zimmer, *Nussbaum*, no. 65.

41. Willi Wolfradt in *Kunst der Zeit*, 1 (1930), nos. 10/11, 249.

42. Gert Schiff, "An Epoch of Longing: An Introduction to German Painting of the Nineteenth Century," in The Metropolitan Museum of Art, *German Masters of the Nineteenth Century* (New York, 1981), 22.

    The significance of the color blue for German Romanticism derives from the poet and novelist Novalis — pseudonym of Friedrich von Hardenberg (1772–1801). One of the pioneers of the Romantic movement, Novalis was the author of *Heinrich von Ofterdingen* (pub. 1802), in which the hero searches for a mysterious blue flower.

43. Hugh Honour, *Romanticism* (New York, 1979), 73–74.

44. See Jörg Traeger, *Philipp Otto Runge und sein Werk: Monographie und kritischer Katalog* (Munich, 1975), 84–86, 378–79.

45. Robert Rosenblum, *Modern Painting and the Northern Romantic Tradition: Friedrich to Rothko* (New York, 1975), 87.

46. Junk and Zimmer, *Nussbaum*, no. 43.

47. *Ibid.*, no. 223.

48. I am reminded of the poem by Wilhelm Müller, "Der Leiermann," well-known as the last song in Franz Schubert's cycle *Die Winterreise*. Though the details are different (Müller wrote of an old barefoot man playing his hurdy-gurdy in the snow, surrounded by snarling dogs), there is something in the overall mood of Müller's poem and Schubert's song that resonates in Nussbaum's painting. The protagonist of *Die Winterreise*, spurned in love, wanders through a desolate winter landscape that reflects his own state of despair and misery. Having rejected suicide, he continues his journey until he discovers the old organ grinder who seems to have calmly accepted his lot:

    Keiner mag ihn hören, keiner sieht ihn an.
    Und die Hunde knurren um den alten Mann.
    Und er lässt es gehen alles wie es will.
    Dreht, und seine Leier steht ihm nimmer still.
    Wunderlicher Alter, soll ich mit dir geh'n?
    Willst zu meinem Liedern deine Leier dreh'n?

    No one wants to hear him, no one looks at him.
    And the dogs snarl around the old man.
    And he lets it all go on as it will.
    He grinds, and his hurdy-gurdy never remains silent.
    Strange old man, shall I go with you?
    Will you grind your hurdy-gurdy to my songs?

49. Émile Langui, "Interviews op Mansarden. Felix Nussbaum: de zachte humor in ballingschap," *Vooruit. Orgaan der Belgische Werkliedenpartij*, no. 35, 5 February 1939, 8. Reprinted in German in Osnabrück, flyer no. 20, "Nussbaum über sich selbst," 31.

50. *Das Kunstblatt*, 15 (1931), no. 5, 159, (ill.). The article is unsigned, but was probably written by Paul Westheim.

51. See Osnabrück, flyer no. 5, "Felix Nussbaum, *Der tolle Pariser Platz*, Berlin, 1931," 5.

52. Junk and Zimmer, *Nussbaum*, 8.

53. Osnabrück, flyer no. 5, 8.

54. See *ibid.*, 9.

55. *Ibid.*, 8.

56. Paul Westheim, "Ausstellungen," *Das Kunstblatt*, 14 (1930), no. 5, 158.

57. Langui, *Vooruit*, 8. Reprinted in Osnabrück, flyer no. 20, 3.

58. Published in Junk and Zimmer, *Nussbaum*, 90 – 91.

59. Osnabrück, flyer no. 8, "Felix Nussbaum, *Zerstörung*, 1933," 5.

60. For an interpretation relating the imagery in this drawing to the biblical story of Joshua and the Battle of Jericho, see *ibid.* The Joshua story is one of military victory that benefited the children of Israel, whereas Nussbaum's drawing seems to be a vision of destruction without any positive indications except for the survival of the couple.

61. *Ibid.*, 5.

62. Junk and Zimmer, *Nussbaum*, 99.

63. See also, for example, *ibid.*, nos. 152, 153, 155, 157, 190 and 200.

64. See *ibid.*, 132 – 34.

65. See Schmied, *Tendenzen*, 4/32 – 33, nos. 4/9 – 11, 4/77 and 4/79.

66. Junk and Zimmer, *Nussbaum*, no. N5.

67. *Ibid.*, 136.

68. Illustrated in Haftmann, *Painting in the Twentieth Century*, II, 309.

69. See Junk and Zimmer, *Nussbaum*, 39 – 40, 59.

70. See Alfred Rubens, *A History of Jewish Costume* (rev. ed.; New York, 1973), 92ff. The *Judenhut* was a symbol of Jewry in Europe for both Jews and non-Jews. See The Jewish Museum, *A Tale of Two Cities*, no. 45.

71. Osnabrück, flyer no. 11, "Belgischen Fremdenpass für Felix Nussbaum, 1935," 6.

72. Dossier text reprinted in Junk and Zimmer, *Nussbaum*, 112.

73. See Frank Patrick Edebau, "James Ensor and Ostend," in The Art Institute of Chicago and The Solomon R. Guggenheim Museum, New York, *Ensor* (New York, 1976), 26.

74. Libby Tannenbaum, *James Ensor. An Iconographic Study*, unpublished M.A. thesis, New York University, Institute of Fine Arts, 1942, 62.

75. Gert Schiff, "James Ensor: *Skeletons in the Studio*," *National Gallery of Canada Annual Bulletin* 4 (1982), 31.

76. See, for example, Adolf Rosenberg, *Adriaen und Isack van Ostade* (Bielefeld and Leipzig, 1900), figs. 28, 29, 37, and 46.

77. Osnabrück, flyer no. 12, "Felix Nussbaum, *Selbstbildnis mit Bruder*, 1937," 6.

78. Junk and Zimmer, *Nussbaum*, nos. 220 – 23.

79. The above interpretation is presented in Osnabrück, flyer no. 12.

80. Nussbaum developed the image of Justus in a large charcoal drawing and a gouache, Junk and Zimmer, *Nussbaum*, nos. 205 and 206.

81. Uta Gerlach-Laxner, *Hans von Marées. Katalog seiner Gemälde* (Munich, 1980), no. 62.

82. For more information, see Osnabrück, flyer no. 10, "Felka Platek (1899 – 1944), Malerin, Lebensgefährtin Felix Nussbaums."

83. *Ibid.*, 6.

84. Junk and Zimmer, *Nussbaum*, no. 216.

85. For related images of alienation between the sexes in the work of Anton Räderscheidt (1892 – 1970), see Joachim Heusinger von Waldegg, "Zur Ikonographie der 'einsamen Paare' bei Anton Räderscheidt," *Pantheon*, 37 (1979), 59 – 68.

86. See Junk and Zimmer, *Nussbaum*, 132.

87. Soby, *De Chirico*, 13. See also, for example, Sironi's *Allieva*, 1929, cover ill., Centre Georges Pompidou, *Les Realismes 1919 – 1939* (Paris, 1981).

88. Giorgio de Chirico, "Sull'arte metafisica," *Valori Plastici*, nos. 4 – 5 (Rome, 1919), 17, published in English translation in Soby, *De Chirico*, 79 – 80.

89. See also Osnabrück, flyer no. 13, "Felix Nussbaum, *Surreale Landschaft*, 1939," 5.

90. See Junk and Zimmer, *Nussbaum*, no. 234 (still life) and no. 225 (self-portrait). Nussbaum also depicted himself with a glove in *Masks and Cat*, 1935, No. 33 in this exhibition.

91. See J. Kirk T. Varnedoe and Elizabeth Streicher, *Graphic Works of Max Klinger* (New York, 1977), XV and pls. 18 – 27.

92. Soby, *De Chirico*, 29. For other appearances of the glove in the work of De Chirico, see ills. on pp. 77, 196, 198, and 231.

93. *Ibid.*, 75 – 76.

94. Nussbaum painted a similar view of Brussels rooftops with an oversized dishtowel hanging in place of the gloves in an oil painting, ca. 1937, Junk and Zimmer, *Nussbaum*, no. 208.

95. Osnabrück, flyer no. 14, 4.

96. See Osnabrück, flyer no. 15, "Felix Nussbaum, *ST. CYPRIEN (Gefangene in Saint-Cyprien)*, 18 Juni 1942," 3.

97. The same man was given a drawing by Karl Schwesig. (See Blatter and Milton, *Art of the Holocaust*, fig. 133.)

98. Scenes of prayer where the *tallit* (prayer shawl) is a prominent motif occur in many works produced in concentration camps. See *ibid.*, figs, 46, 95, 107, and 113.

99. Otto Stelzer, *Paula Modersohn-Becker* (Berlin, 1958), pl. 83.

100. See Schmied, *Tendenzen*, 4/2 – 3, and nos. 4/30, 91 – 92, and 144.

101. Willard Bohn, "Apollinaire and De Chirico: The Making of the Mannequins," *Comparative Literature*, 27 (1975), 158 – 165, especially 164 – 65.

102. See also, Osnabrück, flyer no. 17, "Felix Nussbaum, *Selbstbildnis mit Judenpass*, 1943," 2.

103. For example, *The Daughter of the West*, 1919 and *Metaphysical Muse*, 1917; see *Tendenzen*, 4/3 and no. 4/16.

104. See *ibid.*, no. 4/141.

105. See Osnabrück, flyer no. 20, "Felix Nussbaum, *Die Gerippe Spielen zum Tanz*, 18.4.1944," 1.

106. See Dan Erdmann-Degenhardt and Serge Klarsfeld, "La déportation des juifs de Belgique," *Le Monde Juif. La Revue du Centre de Documentation Juive Contemporaine*, 39 (Jan. – March 1983), no. 109, 30 – 33.

107. See "Totentanz," in *Der Grosse Brockhaus*, 18 (Leipzig, 1934), 777.

108. Osnabrück, flyer no. 20, 4 – 6.

109. Isaiah 32:6, translation The Jewish Publication Society of America, *The Prophets. A New Translation* (Philadelphia, 1978), 423.

THE ARTIST IN EXILE, INTERNMENT AND HIDING

SYBIL MILTON

THE EXODUS of German Jewish artists and intellectuals after 1933 to temporary havens in adjacent countries in continental Europe was unique in scope and impact.[1] Their traumatic flight was the subject of Bertolt Brecht's 1937 poem "Concerning the Label Emigrant,"[2] and was also depicted in Felix Nussbaum's 1940 watercolor *Prisoners at St. Cyprien* (No. 63). The refugees were usually unwelcome as either transients or residents, and remained vulnerable to Nazi measures that denaturalized them, confiscated their works, and stripped them of their professional affiliations. Felix Nussbaum's search for refuge during this decade mirrored the general experiences of his German Jewish compatriots, more than 700 of whom were professional artists.[4]

The emigration during the twelve years of Nazi rule can be divided into three main periods. The first, from the accession to power in January 1933 to the annexation of Austria in March 1938, was characterized by the dislocation of precipitate flight and the attendant loss of social and professional status. The emigrés selected, for the most part, interim residences in nearby central Europe during this period, reflecting a prevalent belief that they would soon be able to return to Germany. This period, the height of the Great Depression, was also a time of widespread anti-intellectualism, anti-Semitism, and xenophobia in most host nations. The second phase, between the *Anschluss* and Pearl Harbor, was marked by increasing Nazi anti-Jewish violence, illegal mass flight, and increasingly restrictive immigration policies, and after the outbreak of war in September 1939, the growing vulnerability of emigrés to forced labor and internment in their temporary European domiciles. The third period, from the invasion of the Soviet Union in 1941 to the defeat of the Third Reich in 1945, culminated in the attempt to exterminate European Jews, with decreasing possibilities of survival or rescue through either flight or hiding.

In January 1933, Nussbaum was already abroad, as a fellowship recipient at the Villa Massimo, the Rome campus of the Prussian Academy of Arts, where he had resided since the previous October. At the end of 1932 his Berlin studio had burned, destroying most of his earlier work. This involuntary severance from his earlier works probably reinforced the impact of his later exclusion as a Jew under newly promulgated racial legislation. Moreover, anti-Semitic incidents directed at Felix Nussbaum at the Villa Massimo coincided with Goebbels' personal visit there in May 1933. Nussbaum was also instantaneously affected by the implementation of the Aryan paragraphs of the Civil Service Law of 7 April 1933, resulting in the cancellation of his fellowship at the end of May. Stipends and grants were considered as academic positions under this legislation.[5] Stripped of his professional affiliation and even the nominal income of a grant, Nussbaum was dependent on parental support. Although he left Rome in May 1933, together with his companion and later wife, Felka Platek, he remained in Italy, staying until the end of 1934 on the Italian Riviera at Alassio and Rapallo.

His continued presence in Italy was attributable to professional expediency and the lenient conditions for refugees in fascist Italy. There was the possibility of sponsorship by Charlotte Berend-Corinth, the widow of the famous German artist Lovis Corinth and an important Impressionist in her own right; she resided in Alassio from 1933 to 1939.[6] Furthermore, Nussbaum's wealthy parents spent much of 1934 in Basel and Rapallo. It is important to remember the pragmatism of Mussolini's Jewish policies before 1938, which enabled 1,200 German Jews to enter Italy as temporary residents by October 1934.[7] Visas were not mandatory, religion did not have to be listed in Italian residence permits, and work permits were obtained with comparative ease during the early 1930s. Furthermore, Italian fascism tolerated most avant-garde art and literature in contrast to Nazi Germany. The Nazis had already staged spectacular public bonfires of books by Jewish authors in May 1933, "the auto-da-fé of a century of German culture."[8] They also banned and villified most modern and Jewish artists, culminating in the Degenerate Art (Entartete Kunst) exhibit in Munich during 1937.[9] In 1935 Nussbaum left Italy and after one month in Switzerland and Paris found refuge in Belgium in early February 1935, his home for the next nine years.

Unlike most other exiled artists, Felix Nussbaum and Felka Platek were relatively affluent, and did not have to accept low-paying odd jobs to make ends meet. Their comfortable lifestyle contrasted strongly with the marginal existence of refugees depicted in Erich Maria Remarque's novel Arch of Triumph.[10] Felix Nussbaum and Felka Platek did not have to depend on occasional sales of paintings on consignment through dealers in order to pay for materials (canvas, paints, and brushes) or studio space; they were self-supporting, with their own substantial savings supplemented by monthly allowances sent by relatives in London.[11]

Nussbaum was neither a political activist nor did he claim racial persecution as grounds for entering Belgium in 1935. Ostensibly a tourist studying the Flemish Old Masters, he initially settled in the seaport of Ostend. He was already familiar with this town from previous visits. Ostend was congenial and Nussbaum was visited there in 1935 by Rudi Lesser, a childhood friend from Osnabrück and a fellow art student in Berlin. Ostend was frequently visited in 1935 by other prominent German literary refugees, such as Ernst Toller, Stefan Zweig, Erwin Egon Kisch, and Hermann Kesten. It was also the place where Joseph Roth and Irmgard Keun met and began their romantic liaison in the mid-1930s.[12] However, after 1936, even relatively prominent literary personalities like Roth and Kesten had difficulty in obtaining limited Belgian transit visas in order to complete their journeys between Paris and Amsterdam.[13] It is not known whether Nussbaum ever met these famous refugees in Ostend.

Despite the presence of fascist movements, democratic Belgium was initially relatively hospitable to German refugees. Approximately 13,000–15,000 German and Austrian Jews found legal asylum in Belgium between January 1933 and September 1938.[14] An additional 3,000 German and Austrian Jewish refugees crossed the border illegally between October and December 1938; this group also included several hundred

63. *Prisoners at St. Cyprien (2)*, 1940

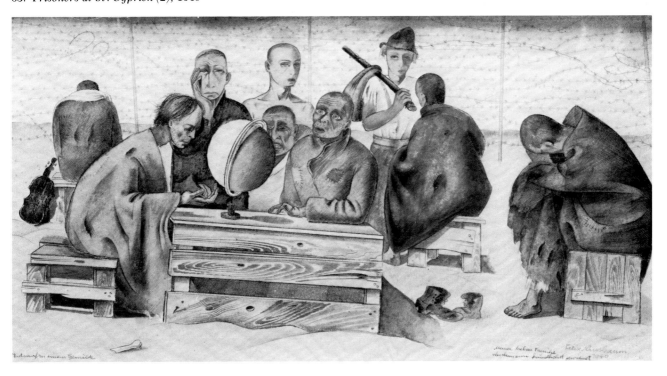

27. *Fisherman's House in Alassio,* 1933

Polish Jews who had resided in Germany. Felka Platek, born in Warsaw in 1899, had moved to Germany as an art student during the mid-1920s; had she not gone to Belgium with Nussbaum it is probable that she would have been expelled from Germany and deported to Poland along with 17,000 other *Ostjuden* on 28 October 1938.[15] The small group of German Jewish refugees resident in Belgium complained about dilatory bureaucratic procedures and increasingly stringent enforcement of immigration regulations by the Belgian police after 1938. The police used administrative techniques such as repatriation and *refoulement* (the police expulsion of illegal immigrants caught within the 15 km. border zone) to expel recent illegal arrivals.[16] Already apprehensive about their future, the refugees felt more vulnerable and exposed when the Belgian police expelled Heinrich Bell, a communist functionary, along with four additional illegal Jewish immigrants, and handed them over to the Gestapo in February 1936. Other incidents, such as the Nazi abduction of the journalist Berthold Jacob from France in March 1935 and Gestapo surveillance of German exiles abroad, increased their fears of entrapment.[17] Moreover, Belgium's geographic and military position as a small country adjacent to Germany reinforced their fears.

Legal residence permits for foreigners were issued in very limited quantities for periods of six months ("white cards") or two years ("yellow cards"). Recipients of white cards were prohibited salaried employment and political activity; the need for constant renewals increased their sense of insecurity. This mandatory semiannual renewal explains Felix Nussbaum's constant changes of address between February 1935 and September 1937, when he moved every six months from Ostend to Brussels (or environs), and vice versa, in order to renew his visa. Felix Nussbaum and Felka Platek both held white cards, even after they settled and married in Brussels in the fall of 1937.

The trauma of exile severed established connections between artists, galleries, and markets. Moreover, national differences in taste and the limitations of the art market in the inauspicious economic climate of the depression increased the difficulties faced by young artists, such as Felix Nussbaum, in obtaining exhibit space or publicity. Analogous to the loss of language confronting refugee writers, the emigré artists also had to reestablish social and professional networks.[18] By 1938–1939, Nussbaum began to receive gallery space in Amsterdam, Paris, and Brussels through the nexus of family connections, fellow refugees, and the sympathetic Belgian socialist press. Several of his watercolors were included in the collective exhibit of November 1938 in Paris entitled "Free German Art" that included works by seventy other exile artists. However, friendly press coverage of the exhibit in the *Pariser Tageszeitung* by Paul Westheim only mentioned Nussbaum in passing.[19] His Belgian friend, the sculptor Dolf Ledel, secured him gallery space in the socialist café Socialist Club 38 in downtown Brussels, where Nussbaum had a show in February 1939. Furthermore, the Belgian art critic, Émile Langui, published a series of articles entitled "Attic Interviews" in the cultural section of the Belgian socialist daily *Vooruit*. The lengthy interview with Felix Nussbaum appeared in early 1939 and also introduced the subject of "exile art":

There is an art that remains unknown. It exists without money, without public acclaim, without publicity, and without sales. . . . It is the art of the banned and homeless German and Austrian refugees, who despite their grumbling stomachs and worn-out shoes still pursue the eternal dream of beauty and truth. . . . Nussbaum's work is imbued with a tender happiness, an innocent grace, and an unstilted naiveté, which includes humor.[20]

Langui's series also publicized another German refugee artist, the communist Karl Schwesig, who, after crossing the border illegally, settled in Antwerp from 1935 to 1940. Schwesig earned a precarious living from the sale of his paintings, lectures about conditions in Nazi Germany, and performances with an itinerant political cabaret troupe. He lived "from sponging free luncheon invitations, hand-me-down clothing, and free sleeping quarters. These things were normally provided by either the Belgian socialists or by Jewish charities. [He] was also assisted by personal friends, fellow German refugees."[21] Unlike Nussbaum, Schwesig was politically active. In 1936, he published the cycle *Schlegelkeller* in Antwerp, which related through prose and pictures his sixteen months of incarceration in Nazi jails. *Schlegelkeller* was the Nazi nickname for the basement of the Schlegel Brewery in Düsseldorf, where prisoners were interrogated, and which also literally meant in German "cellar of beatings."[22] Schwesig also designed posters for Spanish Republican causes and did illustrations for clandestine anti-Nazi literature that was smuggled into Germany.

Reluctant Belgian hospitality to the German refugees ceased with the invasion of Belgium on 10 May 1940. On that date field workers of the New York-based Joint Distribution Committee estimated that 23,000 German and Austrian Jewish refugees resided alongside 70,000 native Belgian Jews.[23] In the panic that accompanied the invasion, the political and racial anti-Nazi exiles were attacked as potential fifth columnists and arrested as enemy aliens. The brutality that accompanied the Belgian military defeat marked a change from a policy of reluctant asylum to one of mass indifference to the fate of German and Austrian refugees. Foreigners of military age in Belgium were herded into cattle cars, behind sealed doors and without food or water, for shipment to the internment camps of southern France.[24] The French camps had been created in late 1938 and early 1939 to house Spanish Republican refugees, their families, and members of the International Brigade.[25] Ultimately these internment camps under French administration became transit camps ruled by the Germans after 1942. The more than sixty camps in southern France became depots through which one-quarter million Jews were sent to their deaths. One of these was St. Cyprien.

In 1939 St. Cyprien was a small fishing village with a population of 1,172. Located along the Mediterranean in the Département Pyrenées-Orientales, about halfway between the Spanish border and Perpignan, it became an overcrowded city of temporary barracks surrounded by electrified barbed wire on one side and the ocean on the other. It was described as Dante's Inferno by Pablo Casals and "the Pyrenées hell-hole" by the writer Walter Mehring.[26] The camp was opened in early February 1939 for 65,000–75,000 Spaniards; about half were released or emigrated during the spring of 1939. At the start of the war in September 1939, the camp population again increased when 15,000 male German and Austrian nationals residing in France were interned. The initial wave of war hysteria made no distinctions between Nazis and anti-Nazi refugees. Many of the more prominent exiles were able to obtain release by December 1939. After the occupation of Belgium in May 1940, a second wave of internment followed, dumping 7,000 male German, Austrian, and Polish Jews from Belgium into the overcrowded barracks of St. Cyprien. Resident alien women were not arrested in Belgium, although in France they were incarcerated and added to the population of the southern camps. Thus Felka Platek remained in Brussels throughout the summer of 1940, when Felix Nussbaum, Karl Schwesig, and others (like the Austrian refugee artist Kurt Conrad Loew) were transported from Belgium to St. Cyprien.[27] St. Cyprien was closed in late October 1940, when floods wiped out the minimal barracks facilities, and the remaining prisoners were transferred to Gurs and other southern French transit camps.

A ten-page report by an anonymous caseworker was sent to the New York headquarters of the Joint Distribution Committee; it described the plight of those Belgian refugees trapped between 10 May and 30 July 1940.[28] It also contained a graphic description of conditions in St. Cyprien as Felix Nussbaum must have experienced them:

Obtaining visas and other documents have caused me to travel considerably in unoccupied France. It is during these journeys that little by little, I found traces of our refugees and made contact with them, as well as with thousands of those who became refugees since May 1940.

In a short time, I was able to ascertain that a very large part of the refugees formerly assisted by the Belgian Committee are now in France in precarious situations. It was only when I visited the camp at St. Cyprien that I fully realized the disaster which has befallen these unfortunate souls, who had already been so sorely tried. . . .

The camp at St. Cyprien is situated on a beach, about 15 km. from Perpignan and the same distance from the Spanish frontier. It was constructed for the Spaniards interned in France after the victory of Franco, and received the very characteristic nickname, Inferno (Hell) of St. Cyprien. It is a beach about 5 km. long and 200–300 meters wide, surrounded and traversed by long rows of barbed wire. The only vegetation, the telegraph poles! The barracks are of planks, poorly jointed, covered with corrugated iron and without boards underneath. Several narrow windows, placed near the roofs, are clearly insufficient to ventilate a barrack where 80 people sleep, at 25 cm. space one from the other, in two rows a meter apart, on straw which is placed directly on the sand. No furniture whatsoever, just a few boxes in the barracks. During summer the heat on this beach, situated between the mountains, and completely exposed to the sun from dawn to dusk, is insupportable. In order to hide from the scorching rays of the sun, there are only the overheated barracks, where one suffocates on entering.

The refugees walk about entirely nude, or wearing only shorts, from morning to night. On the other hand, they shiver at night, for it is very cool. Sanitary installations are nonexistent. No light in the barracks, no dining quarters. The refugees eat crouched on their beds. There are naturally no dishes, but bowls made of tin cans. No library, no newspapers. Except for the few who work in the kitchens and on clean-up squads, the refugees have had nothing to do for months, except play cards. When I visited the camp (July 1940), the living conditions were by far better than they had been several weeks previously. The food had become somewhat more satisfactory and more abundant; efforts to keep the place clean had been successful, to some extent. After superhuman efforts, I may say, medical service had been organized, and some indispensible medicines had been obtained, so that an epidemic of intestinal grippe, from which practically all the inhabitants of the camp had suffered, was checked. The refugees received permission to bathe in the sea and this markedly improved the hygienic conditions of the camp.

But the living conditions in St. Cyprien before the armistice and during the subsequent weeks, were really frightful, according to many witnesses; a loaf of bread was distributed among ten persons per day (100 grams per person);* coffee in the morning and evening and a bowl of bean soup, most often without meat, at noon. Everyone was terribly hungry; the canteen which is not functioning any too well now, did not exist and the refugees were scandalously exploited by the soldiers of the guard, as well as unfortunately by some sorry inhabitants of St. Cyprien itself. At that time, a bar of chocolate sold for 50 francs, a cigarette at 20 francs, a newspaper at 50 francs, a loaf of bread weighing 1 kg. at 200 francs, a postage stamp at 20 times its face value, etc., etc. If we add to this the fact that the Belgian franc, the only currency in the possession of most of the refugees, was exchanged at the rate of 500 Belgian francs for 100 French francs, the picture is complete!

. . . It is evident that the living conditions of the refugees at St. Cyprien are unbearable and almost surpass the limits of human endurance. But all these physical privations, no matter how painful, are nothing compared to the moral distress which reigns at St. Cyprien, as probably at the other camps, too.

There was an active cultural life despite overcrowding, undernourishment, and epidemics (dysentery, typhoid, and malaria), and the alternating indifference, corruption, and sporadic brutality of the French soldiers and policemen guarding St. Cyprien. Twenty-three unnamed Spanish artists were in Argèles-sur-mer and St. Cyprien in late 1939. Although neither their identities nor their works survived, information exists about the mediums they worked in. They used "driftwood, low-grade clay, the canvas walls of tents (for murals), and squares of wood polished with sand (for carved woodcuts)."[29] The refugee artists of St. Cyprien during the summer of 1940 included at least two Germans, Felix Nussbaum and Karl Schwesig; one Austrian, Kurt Conrad Loew; and one Polish refugee, Osias Hofstaetter.[30] It is known that Karl Schwesig completed more than 300 sketches and watercolors in St. Cyprien; many works portrayed the grimmer aspects of his daily life and camp routines, depicting improvised medical care, the mortuary, disinfection, daily hygiene, barracks' interiors, and so forth. Many works were portraits of fellow internees; these preserved and immortalized the presence of the sitter, and were especially important when temporal physical existence was fragile and survival tenuous. Artistic self-discipline and work occupied time and was a way of combatting the demoralization and ennui of internment. Occasionally, it also provided reinforcement of the will to survive and to resist.[31] Nussbaum portrayed the plight of the dispossessed refugees and also sketched the camp synagogue (see Nos. 61–64). Loew focused on the distribution of food and the omnipresence of hunger. All did self-portraits of their plight as professional artists in internment.[32] Although reports of exhibits in Gurs and Compiègne exist, it is not known

105. Felix Nussbaum's alien registration card

*In the surviving art from St. Cyprien during 1940, Kurt Conrad Loew sketched the division of a loaf of bread between six men, showing the weighing of individual portions.

Eine Zeitung ist im Lager eingetroffen. Ein Internierter liest seinen Kameraden daraus vor. Niedergeschlagenheit, Resignation und Verzweiflung spiegeln sich in den Gesichtern und der Haltung der Zuhörer wieder.
Un prisonnier s'est procuré un journal. Il lit les nouvelles à ses camarades.

Die Gefangenen von St. Cyprien

Aufnahmen aus einem Interniertenlager in Südfrankreich

Nur ein paar resümierende, aber bezeichnende Sätze aus dem umfangreichen Bericht eines Insassen im südfranzösischen Interniertenlager St. Cyprien können wir hier zu diesen Bildern wiedergeben: «Dicht beieinander wohnen an den Gestaden des Mittelmeeres Glück und Unglück. Da erlebt man Tage voll von dem Zauber dieser einmaligen Verbindung von südländischem Glanz und alpiner Herbheit; aber gibt es für Menschen etwas Schlimmeres als aus dem normalen Leben, aus der Arbeit herausgerissen zu sein und auch nicht die Möglichkeit eines Versuches zu haben, gegen diesen Strom zu schwimmen? Es ist das Schlimmste, was eine Gefangenschaft mit sich bringt: auf alles verzichten müssen, was einem seit frühester Jugend Selbstverständlichkeit geworden war. Dazu sind alle Imponderabilien, die so ein Lager umgeben, so gravierend, daß Sonne und azurblaues Meer dahinter verblassen. Bedenkt man noch, daß die Internierten fast alle Familienväter sind, deren Frauen und Kinder getrennt in andern Lagern Frankreichs untergebracht sind, so scheint es begreiflich, daß der Drang nach der Freiheit mitunter zu einer Art Psychose wird. Manche, die ein Leben lang kaum einen Wunsch unerfüllt sahen, denen ein glückliches Geschick die Sorgen ums tägliche Brot erspart, schlafen hier in karg gestreutem Stroh auf dem Sandboden einer primitiven Holzbaracke und essen aus angerosteten Blechtöpfen, die früher mit Wurstkonserven gefüllt waren. Die im Lager fehlende Lichtanlage ist notdürftig durch Kerzenbeleuchtung ersetzt, das Trinkwasser fehlt und die Gefahr der Infektions- und Magenkrankheiten bedeutet für alle Internierten eine wahre Zerreißprobe. Viele von uns, die beim ersten Antreten mit einem ‚präsent' antworteten, werden, wenn einst die doppelten Stacheldrahtschranken fallen, fehlen und ihre letzte Ruhestätte im Sand am Meeresstrand gefunden haben, gleich wie die Flüchtlinge aus Spanien, die hier im Frühjahr 1939 der Erschöpfung, der Ruhr, dem Typhus, der Malaria oder dem Heimweh erlegen sind.»
                                                                                                                        Spectator

Les prisonniers de St-Cyprien

Au début des hostilités tous les étrangers qui ne purent justifier de leur présence en France, furent internés dans des camps. Nombreux sont parmi eux les suspects, les indésirables, les agitateurs, les réfugiés chassés du IIIme Reich. Il y eut également des erreurs judiciaires, tel de nos compatriotes devait en être victime, qui relata dans les colonnes de la «Gazette de Lausanne» l'horreur d'une telle captivité. A St-Cyprien, dans le sud de la France, est situé l'un de ces camps d'internement. Les prisonniers logent dans des baraques de planches, qui n'ont pas de plancher. Ils couchent sur la paille disposée à même le sable humide, mangent dans des boîtes de conserve rouillées, s'éclairent à la bougie. Il n'y a pas d'eau potable dans le camp et l'état de saleté des détenus est un constant danger d'infection. Aux misères physiques s'ajoutent les misères morales, les brimades, dont les prisonniers sont l'objet et l'ignorance, où ils sont tenus du sort des leurs, de leurs femmes, de leurs enfants, internés dans d'autres camps. Quels que soient les crimes dont ils sont accusés, on ne peut s'empêcher de les plaindre.

Nr. 47 · 1940 Seite 1288

Morgenappell vor der Baracke.
L'appel du matin devant les baraquements.

110. "The Prisoners of St. Cyprien," photo essay in *Zürcher Illustrierte*, 22 November, 1940

whether the internees were also able to mount similar exhibits in St. Cyprien during 1940.[33] Since only about seventeen percent of the art created in internment and transit camps survived, it is probable that the full range of art in St. Cyprien was wider than can be documented.

Art was legal and materials were available in St. Cyprien and the other French internment camps during 1940 and 1941. This contrasts favorably with conditions in the camps and ghettos in eastern and central Europe, where only clandestine art existed and artists had to depend on improvised and filched materials. In St. Cyprien, the Red Cross, the American Friends Service Committee, Joint Distribution Committee, and other relief agencies provided paper, paints, inks, and pencils. Artists also brought small sketch pads with them, as well as pastels or watercolors. Although art materials were not plentiful they were most certainly available, since the French authorities saw culture as a way of keeping prisoners busy. After Nussbaum had left St. Cyprien and the inmates were transferred to Gurs in late October 1940, paper supplies became scarcer. At first, artists in Gurs improvised, using school children's notebooks, as did Hans Reichel, and the perforated blank margins of postage stamps, as did Karl Schwesig. His use of a miniaturist's technique enabled Schwesig to cram the maximum amount of information on the smallest-size paper, which could then be hidden and smuggled out of the camp.[34] It is probable that similar types of art were also created at St. Cyprien.

Art was also often bartered for food, clothing, better quarters, or more lenient work assignments. Occasionally art was used as barter for securing passes into adjacent towns, a trip that offered potential escape routes. Thus Max Ernst gave the commandant of Les Milles twenty-seven of his paintings, which the latter sold for 500 French francs; this enabled Ernst to pick up his emergency visa for the United States.[35] Drawings shown at the two exhibits held in Gurs in 1940 and 1941 were sold to the local populace, as reported in Hanna Schramm's memoirs. Artworks were also given as presents to fellow inmates and to the relief workers who tried to ameliorate the miserable conditions of the internment camps.

Almost all the internment camps in southern France also had active adult-education programs as well as schools for the children. Studio art and art history were both taught. It is probable that St. Cyprien conformed to this general pattern, since it was believed that Schwesig taught Hofstaetter art during their internment.[36] Theatrical performances, cabarets, and concerts were also available in almost all of the camps, as was language instruction and the possibility of religious worship. The

situation in St. Cyprien probably followed the example of Gurs in the cultural profusion that developed.

Nussbaum escaped from St. Cyprien after two-and-one-half months internment there. Under Article 19 of the Franco-German armistice signed on 26 June 1940, a delegation of German diplomatic and police officials, known as the Kundt Commission, was allowed to visit the internment camps in the unoccupied south to designate those German nationals who would be repatriated. The commission arrived in St. Cyprien during the first week of August. For racial and political opponents of Nazi Germany this brought the renewed danger of immediate deportation to concentration camps, since only Nazis or Aryans could return to Germany. Despite the risks it entailed, Felix Nussbaum, accompanied by his Osnabrück childhood friend, Georg Mayer, requested repatriation. Nussbaum and Mayer were sent in mid-August 1940 with the second convoy from St. Cyprien to Germany via a Bordeaux barracks. At this transfer point they escaped by bribing a local milkman whose delivery route included the barracks. They subsequently arrived in Brussels via Paris by taking Red Cross trains. Their luck held, despite the frequent identity checks of civilians on trains in occupied northern France.[37] Escapes were not uncommon from the French camps as late as 1941, when the Austrian-born Jean Améry also fled from Gurs via occupied northern France to Brussels.[38]

Having escaped the Nazi dragnet that trapped many German and Austrian Jews in southern France, Nussbaum confronted the new situation in occupied Belgium ruled by a Belgian civilian government under German military administration. By June 1942 Nussbaum went into hiding with the help of personal friends. Although without money, he obtained from various friends both a small clandestine basement apartment and an attic studio at different Brussels addresses; neither friend knew both addresses. The greatest risks came during the walk between his apartment and his studio, when he was vulnerable to being accidentally caught in Nazi roundups. His isolation and fear were described by other German Jews hiding in Brussels after 1942:

During the night the Gestapo surround whole blocks and search every house for Jews, pack those they find on lorries and steal all their property. A Jewess who lived next door to us was caught in the street, and in her rage revealed that there were still more Jews in the house. The Gestapo came and cleared the whole house. We are in a trap. Fortunately nobody in the street knows us and nobody knows that we are Jews.[39]

Aside from the necessity of eluding the authorities, other fears in hiding included the need to obtain both food and heating fuel (usually coal); ration cards for such necessities were contingent on registration. Nussbaum's friends also provided supplies like canvas and paints after 1942; before that date he could purchase them. Nevertheless, painting in hiding also increased the risks of discovery, because of the noticeable odors of oil paint and turpentine.

Although Nussbaum initially registered under the first anti-Jewish decree of 28 October 1940, he no longer reported in mid-1941 for the census conducted by the *Association des Juifs en Belgique* (AJB), the *Judenrat* for occupied Belgium. Noncompliance with the registration requirements was common, and it was estimated by the German military that approximately 13,000 Jews, at the very least, never completed their registration questionnaires. This was made possible, at least in part, through the support of the Belgian population.[40] The German military administration of Belgium furthermore reported in their 16 March 1942 periodic summary of events that the introduction of the Jewish star had been postponed because it was assumed that the measure would produce a wave of sympathy in an otherwise indifferent Belgian population.[41]

Neither Nussbaum nor Felka Platek survived in the end, although they had made it for four years with the help of a network of courageous prewar friends who provided food, money, hideouts, and painting supplies. Through their help, Felix Nussbaum was even able to earn a small amount of money in hiding by painting ceramics and illustrating schoolbooks.[42] Similarly, the German refugee artist, Tony Simon-Wolfskehl, also hidden in a friend's attic, sold charcoal sketches through her friend's mediation in order to provide money for food and art supplies.[43] Survival in hiding thus depended on the ability to pass as natives in language, manner, and appearance, but also on luck or accident. This became more difficult as German measures intensified during the occupation. Furthermore, those who helped Jews were executed, whereas informers were rewarded with cash, brandy, sugar, or cigarettes.

Almost every Jew here lives in hiding. Nobody knows where anyone stays and it is difficult to keep up contacts. During the day I hardly go out, and if I have to, I scan every car carefully. The police cars can be recognized from afar, and whenever I see one I am seized by deadly fear. We are outlaws. There is a price on the head of every Jew: 500 francs for a Jewish man, 300 francs for a Jewish woman. I never knew what precious possessions freedom and human rights were.[44]

Despite the enormous odds, several thousand German Jews did survive illegally in Belgium, although in the end the Nussbaums were denounced.[45]

In October 1941 the transit camp at Malines (Mechelen) was opened to concentrate the Jews of Belgium. Over 25,000 were eventually deported from Malines directly to Auschwitz between August 1942 and July 1944. One month before liberation, on the last transport of 563 men, women, and children from Malines to Auschwitz, Felix Nussbaum and Felka Platek were deported. As prisoners 284 and 285 they left Malines on 31 July 1944, and arrived in Auschwitz on 3 August 1944. The Nussbaums were not among the 223 men and 138 women that survived the selection on the Birkenau railroad siding.[46]

Felix Nussbaum's brother and his parents had emigrated to Amsterdam. His brother was sent via Westerbork to Auschwitz in early September 1944, and subsequently transferred to Stutthof at the end of October, where he died in early December. Nussbaum's parents were deported via Westerbork to Auschwitz in early February 1944, where they both perished.[47] All Felix Nussbaum's paintings in his parents' Amsterdam home were lost.

The triumph of Nazism in 1933 deprived Felix Nussbaum of his home and career in his native Germany. During his exile in Italy and Belgium, where he shared the uncertain future of other emigrés, he started his career as a young artist for a second time; Felka Platek's career, however, was totally destroyed in exile. Deported to the southern French camps after the invasion of Belgium, Nussbaum escaped and returned to Brussels, where he and his wife survived for four years in hiding. In each phase of his tragic odyssey, his life paralleled the fate of his Jewish contemporaries whose story he told in his art. He perished shortly before liberation, but his unique works survived to tell the story of exile, incarceration, hiding, and death.

NOTES

1. See Jarrel C. Jackman and Carla M. Borden, eds., *The Muses Flee Hitler: Cultural Transfer and Adaptation, 1930–1945* (Washington, D.C., 1983).

2. Bertolt Brecht, "Über die Bezeichnung Emigranten," *Die neue Weltbühne* (Paris), 30 December 1937; translated in Bertolt Brecht, *Poems, 1913–1956*, ed. John Willett, Ralph Mannheim, and Erich Fried (New York, 1976), 301.

3. Herbert A. Strauss, "The Movement of People in a Time of Crisis," in *The Muses Flee Hitler*, 45.

4. *Ibid.*, 54. See also Herbert A. Strauss and Werner Röder, eds., *International Biographical Dictionary of Central European Emigrés, 1933–1945*, vol. 2: *The Sciences and the Arts* (New York and Munich, 1983); Herbert A. Strauss, "Jewish Emigration from Nazi Germany: Nazi Policies and Jewish Responses," *Leo Baeck Institute Yearbook* 25 (1980), 313–61, and *ibid.*, 26 (1981), 343–409; Frederick V. Grunfeld, *Prophets without Honour* (New York, 1979); and Janet Blatter and Sybil Milton, *Art of the Holocaust* (New York, 1981).

5. Peter Junk and Wendelin Zimmer, *Felix Nussbaum: Leben und Werk* (Cologne and Bramsche, 1982), 90–108. Under the 7 April

110. "The Prisoners of St. Cyprien," photo essay in *Zürcher Illustrierte*, 22 November, 1940

1933 Civil Service Law, Max Liebermann, and Käthe Kollwitz were forced to resign from the Prussian Academy of Arts. Liebermann was forced to resign in early May 1933. Kollwitz was compelled to leave in February 1933 and was prohibited from exhibiting (*Ausstellungsverbot*) after 1936.

6. Charlotte Berend-Corinth (b. 1880, Berlin – d. 1967, New York) was an important German Impressionist and graphic artist, who fled Nazi Germany in 1933. She lived in Italy until 1939, when she emigrated to New York.

7. German literary refugee authors in Italy after 1933 included Walter Hasenclever, Alfred Neumann, and Armin T. Wegner. Hasenclever lived in Florence from 1937 to 1939, Neumann from 1933 to 1938. Wegner moved to Rome in April 1934, upon his release from Oranienburg concentration camp; he was arrested for an open letter addressed to Hitler protesting the April 1933 boycott. Wegner also wrote several short stories about the Armenian massacres he had witnessed as a medic during the First World War. See Jürgen Serke, *Die verbrannten Dichter* (Frankfurt, 1980), 55 – 73 and 301 – 06; also Armin T. Wegner, *Die Verbrechen der Stunde, die Verbrechen der Ewigkeit* (Hamburg, 1982). For further information on fascist Italy and Jewish refugees, see Klaus Voigt, "Exil in Italien," in Edith Böhne and Wolfgang Motzkau-Valeton, eds., *Aspekte des Exils: Beiträge zur Woche der verbrannten Bücher in Osnabrück* (2 vols.; Heidelberg: Lambert Schneider, in press), courtesy of Dr. Voigt, West Berlin; also Meier Michaelis, *Mussolini and the Jews: German-Italian Relations and the Jewish Question in Italy, 1922–1945* (London and Oxford, 1978); Meier Michaelis, "The Attitude of the Fascist Regime to Jews in Italy," *Yad Vashem Studies* 4 (1960), 7 – 41; and Guido Valebrega, ed., *Gli Ebrei in Italia durante il Fascismo*, 2 (Milan and Turin, 1962), and *ibid.*, 3 (1963).

8. Karl Dietrich Bracher, *The German Dictatorship: The Origins, Structure and Effects of National Socialism*, trans. Jean Steinberg (New York and Washington, D.C., 1970), 258.

9. Bertold Hinz, *Art in the Third Reich* (New York, 1979); and Sybil Milton, "Artists in the Third Reich," in Henry Friedlander and Sybil Milton, eds., *The Holocaust: Ideology, Bureaucracy and Genocide; the San Jose Papers* (Millwood, New York, 1981), 115 – 29.

10. Erich Maria Remarque, *Arch of Triumph* (New York, 1947). Remarque and Nussbaum were both natives of Osnabrück.

11. Brussels, Belgian Ministry of Justice, Resident Aliens' Register: Case File 146129, Felix Nussbaum and Felka Platek; photocopies courtesy of Karl Zeilinger, Director of Service Social Juif, Brussels.

12. Ernst Toller (b. 1893, Samotschin, Posen – d. 1939 suicide, New York) was an author and dramatist whose name was on the first Nazi denaturalization list in 1933 for his participation in the Munich revolutionary government of 1918 – 1919. During the 1930s he attended the International Congress of Writers for the Defense of Culture in July 1938 in Paris and actively protested Nazi cultural policies in public speeches, radio programs, books, and articles. Stefan Zweig was an Austrian Jewish author (b. 1881, Vienna – d. 1942 suicide, Petropolis, Brazil). Erwin Egon Kisch was a journalist (b. 1885, Prague – d. 1948, Prague), who emigrated to France in 1933, where he was an active antifascist. Hermann Kesten (b. 1900, Podwoloczyska, Galicia, Austria – today resides in Italy) was an author and journalist who emigrated to Paris in 1933. He was the editor of both Allert de Lange and Querido publishing houses in Amsterdam, who printed works by many of the famous literary refugees of the 1930s. He was cofounder of the Union of Free Press and Literature in 1935 and the Association of Independent German Writers and Journalists. In May 1940 he moved to New York; and after the war he emigrated to Italy in 1952. Joseph Roth (b. 1894, Brody, Galicia, Austria – d. 1939, Paris) was a prominent Austrian Jewish author and journalist, active in Austrian legitimist politics. His novels included *Radetzkymarsch*. Irmgard Keun (b. 1914 – today resides in Bonn) was a popular actress and novelist. In 1933, she was suspended from all professional activities for her refusal to join the *Reichs-schriftumskammer*; her books were banned and she was also arrested by the Gestapo. She fled Germany and was Roth's common-law wife from 1936 to 1938. In 1940 she returned to Germany and survived with forged papers. Her light fiction included satiric comments on contemporary affairs. Serke, *Die verbrannten Dichter*, 8 – 31 and 222 – 29.

13. Hans-Albert Walter, *Asylpraxis und Lebensbedingungen in Europa: Deutsche Exilliteratur, 1933 – 1950* (Darmstadt and Neuwied, 1972), 56; and Hermann Kesten, ed., *Deutsche Literatur in Exil: Briefe europäischer Autoren, 1933 – 1949* (Frankfurt, 1973), 61.

14. See Betty Garfinkels, *Belgique, terre d'accueil: Problème du Réfugié, 1933 – 1940* (Brussels, 1974); and John Hope Simpson, *The Refugee Problem: Report of a Survey* (London, New York, and Toronto, 1939), 256 – 57, 353 – 55, and 599 – 600.

15. See Sybil Milton, "The Expulsion of Polish Jews from Germany, October 1938-July 1939: A Documentation," *Leo Baeck Institute Yearbook* 29 (1984), 169 – 99.

16. Simpson, *The Refugee Problem*, 246 – 61 and 574 – 75.

17. See Kurt R. Grossmann, *Emigration: Geschichte der Hitler-Flüchtlinge, 1933 – 1945* (Frankfurt, 1969), 83 – 88; and Herbert E. Tutas, *Nationalsozialismus und Exil: Die Politik des Dritten Reiches gegenüber der deutschen politischen Emigration, 1933 – 1939* (Munich and Vienna, 1975), 66 – 98 and 138 – 203.

18. Helene Maimann, "Sprachlosigkeit: Ein zentrales Phänomen der Exilerfahrung," in *Leben in Exil: Probleme der Integration deutscher Flüchtlinge im Ausland, 1933 – 1945*, ed. Wolfgang Frühwald and Wolfgang Schieder (Hamburg, 1981), 31 – 38.

19. Paul Westheim, "Die Ausstellung des Freien Künstlerbundes in der Maison de la Culture," *Pariser Tageszeitung*, no. 835, 6 – 7 November 1938 and *ibid.*, "Rundgang durch die deutsche Kunstausstellung in der Maison de la Culture," *Pariser Tageszeitung*, no. 837, 9 November 1938, reproduced in *Widerstand statt Anpassung: Deutsche Kunst im Widerstand gegen den Faschismus, 1933 – 1945*, ed. Badischer Kunstverein, Karlsruhe and Elefanten Press (Berlin, 1980), 140.

20. Kulturgeschichtliches Museum, Osnabrück, *Informationsblätter und Postkarten zur Dauerausstellung Felix Nussbaum und die Zeit 1904 – 1944*, ed. Eva Berger, Peter Junk, Karl Georg Kaster, and Wendelin Zimmer (Bramsche, 1983/4), flyer no. 20, "Nussbaum über sich selbst," reprinting the autobiographical interview incorporated in Émile Langui, "Interviews in Dachkammern: Felix Nussbaum, der zarte Humor im Exil," *Vooruit*, no. 35, 5 February 1939.

21. Herbert Remmert and Karl Barth, eds., *Karl Schwesig: Leben und Werk* (Berlin and Düsseldorf, 1984), 81 – 86. Schwesig (b. 1898, Gelsenkirchen – d. 1955, Düsseldorf) was active in the Rheinland Secession during the late 1920s, and in 1933 was secretary of the *Reichsverbandes bildenden Künstler*. Three of his paintings were confiscated by Nazi thugs at the time of his arrest; these works were subsequently attacked in the local Nazi press and later burned in the incinerator of the Düsseldorf Art Academy.

22. Karl Schwesig, *Schlegelkeller*, ed. Gallery Remmert and Barth (Berlin and Düsseldorf, 1983).

23. "Refugees im Kriegsgebiet," *Aufbau* no. 20, 17 May 1940 (New York), 1.

24. The arrest of German Jewish refugees in Brussels and conditions during the journey to southern France are described in a three-page typed letter by the Orthodox rabbi Max Ansbacher, 16 September 1940, transmitted via the Joint Distribution Committee staff in Lyons to headquarters in New York. See Archives of the Joint Distribution Committee (hereafter abbreviated as JDC). Similar reports are found in the memoir collection of the Leo

Baeck Institute, New York (hereafter abbreviated as LBI, NY). See Ernest Simon, "Mein Weg von Brüssel nach Havana, 10. Mai 1940 – 8. Januar 1942," (New York, 1970), a 20-page typed memoir detailing the separation from his wife and children after being arrested in Brussels and the appalling conditions on arrival in St. Cyprien.

25. See Michael R. Marrus and Robert O. Paxton, *Vichy France and the Jews* (New York, 1981), 64 – 67; Louis Stein, *Beyond Death and Exile: The Spanish Republicans in France* (Cambridge, Mass., 1979), 55 – 65; and Gilbert Badia, *et al.*, *Les barbelés de l'exil: Études sur l'émigration allemande et autrichienne, 1938 – 1940* (Grenoble, 1979).

26. Pablo Casals, *Joys and Sorrows* (New York, 1970), 233; and Walter Mehring, *Wir müssen weiter* (Düsseldorf, 1979), 85 and 125f.

27. Blatter and Milton, *Art of the Holocaust*, 36 – 39, 102 – 13, 256, 260, and 263. Reports about conditions in Gurs, St. Cyprien, Rivesaltes, Nexon, Noé, Les Milles, and Le Vernet are located in the archives of the LBI and JDC in New York and the archives of the American Friends Service Committee in Philadelphia. Published literature about the internment camps in Vichy France by contemporaries included: about Le Vernet: Arthur Koestler, *Scum of the Earth* (New York, 1941); about Les Milles: Lion Feucht–wanger, *The Devil in France* (London, n.d.), reissued under the original title *Der Teufel in Frankreich: Ein Erlebnisbericht* (Munich and Vienna, 1983); and about St. Cyprien: in the memoirs of Alfred Kantorowicz, *Exil in Frankreich* (Bremen, 1971), 197 and the illustrated news story, "Die Gefangenen von St. Cyprien," *Zürcher Illustrierte*, no. 47, 22 November 1940, 1288 – 89, see No. 110 in this exhibition.

28. JDC: Files on German refugees in France, 10-page unsigned single-spaced report about Belgian refugees in St. Cyprien written by a member of the JDC Brussels office, 26 September 1940, 4 – 6. Special thanks to the JDC archivist, Mrs. Rose Klepfisz, who made this material available.

29. Stein, *Beyond Death and Exile*, 93 – 94 and 105.

30. Karl Schwesig completed a portrait of Hofstaetter (b. 1905, Poland – today resides in Israel). Hofstaetter was interned in St. Cyprien and Gurs, eventually escaping to Switzerland and finally immigrating to Israel after the war. Many of Hofstaetter's works are in the collections of the Kibbutz Lochamei HaGhettaot (the Ghetto Fighters Kibbutz) in Israel. Kurt Conrad Loew (b. 1914, Vienna – d. 1980 Vienna) arrived in Belgium in 1939. Interned in St. Cyprien and Gurs from 1940 to 1942, he escaped to Switzerland late in 1942. His literary and artistic estate is located in the collections of the Documentation Archives of the Austrian Resistance in Vienna.

31. Over 300 works by Schwesig from St. Cyprien are located in the Kibbutz Lochamei HaGhettaot in Israel; a list of these works is located in the literary and artistic estate of Karl Schwesig owned by the Gallery Remmert and Barth in Düsseldorf. The surviving papers include an autobiographical manuscript of 83 typed pages written in 1948, subsequently entitled "der Pyrenäen-Bericht." See Remmert and Barth, *Karl Schwesig*, 87 – 97.

32. Blatter and Milton, *Art of the Holocaust*, see Note 24, above.

33. Hanna Schramm, *Menschen in Gurs*, ed. Barbara Vormeier (Worms, 1977), 119 – 26 and the history of Compiègne published by Jean-Jacques Bernard, *Le camp de la morte lente* (Paris, 1944). Bernard was the only Jew not deported from Compiègne. See also Blatter and Milton, *Art of the Holocaust*, 96.

34. See Remmert and Barth, *Karl Schwesig*, 91 – 96; also Blatter and Milton, *Art of the Holocaust, passim.*

35. *Widerstand statt Anpassung*, 148 – 53.

36. French Foreign Office and Goethe Institute, *Deutsche Emigranten in Frankreich; Französische Emigranten in Deutschland, 1685 – 1945* (Paris, 1983), 157 – 158. See also, Hermann Langbein, *Die Stärkeren: Ein Bericht aus Auschwitz und anderen Konzentrationslagern* (Cologne, 1982), 16 – 54, especially 30 – 32 about the adult education "school" in Gurs. See also, Blatter and Milton, *Art of the Holocaust, passim.*

37. Junk and Zimmer, *Nussbaum*, 148 – 49.

38. Jean Améry, *Örtlichkeiten* (Stuttgart, 1980), 49 – 69.

39. LBI, NY, Max Kreutzberger Research Papers, AR 7183, Box 8, folder 1. This quote is from the manuscript by Paula Littauer, "My Experiences during the Persecution of the Jews in Berlin and Brussels, 1939 – 1945," written in London, October 1945, for the series of Jewish survivors' reports collected by the Jewish Central Information Office, p. 13.

40. Serge Klarsfeld and Maxime Steinberg, eds., *Die Endlösung der Judenfrage in Belgien: Dokumente* (Paris and New York, n.d.), 55 – 57; also Maxime Steinberg, *1942: Les Cent Jours de la Déportation des Juifs de Belgique* (Brussels, 1984); *ibid.*, *La Question Juive, 1940 – 1942* (Brussels, 1983); and Maxime Steinberg, "The Trap of Legality: The Association of the Jews in Belgium," in *Patterns of Jewish Leadership in Nazi Europe, 1933 – 1945: Proceedings of the Third Yad Vashem International Historical Conference* (Jerusalem, 1979), 353 – 76. See also *Die Endlösung der Judenfrage in Belgien: Prozess vor dem Landgericht Kiel, Urteil vom 8. Juli 1981; Beschluss des Bundesgerichtshofs vom 23. März 1982* (Brussels, 1982).

41. Steinberg and Klarsfeld, *Die Endlösung der Judenfrage in Belgien*, 20 – 21.

42. Junk and Zimmer, *Nussbaum*, 150 – 154.

43. Blatter and Milton, *Art of the Holocaust*, 264.

44. LBI, NY: Paul Littauer manuscript, 15 – 16.

45. Similar stories of rescue, either provisionally or until liberation, in Belgium, are found in: Kurt Grossmann, *Die unbesungenen Helden* (Berlin, 1961), 225 – 41. See also Perry London, "The Rescuers: Motivational Hypotheses about Christians who saved Jews from the Nazis," in *Altruism and Helping Behavior: Social Psychological Studies of Some Antecedents and Consequences*, ed. J. Macaulay and L. Berkowitz (New York and London, 1970), 241 – 50.

46. Letter from Dr. A. Opitz, director of the International Tracing Service, to Dr. Peter Junk, 17 July 1979; courtesy of Dr. Peter Junk, City Librarian, Osnabrück.

47. *Ibid.*

CHRONOLOGY

	FELIX NUSSBAUM	FAMILY	RELATED EVENTS
1899	January 3: birth of Fajga (Felka) Platek in Warsaw		
1900		Marriage of Philipp Nussbaum and Rahel van Dyk, Felix's parents	
		Establishment of Gossels & Nussbaum hardware business in Osnabrück	
1901		March: birth of Justus Nussbaum, Felix's older brother	
1904	December 11: birth of Felix Nussbaum in Osnabrück		

1904–1922: CHILDHOOD IN OSNABRÜCK

	FELIX NUSSBAUM	FAMILY	RELATED EVENTS
1906			September: dedication of new synagogue in Osnabrück
1910–1918	Attended Jewish elementary school and gymnasium in Osnabrück		
1914–1918		Growth of family ironworks firm	World War I
1922	Summer: left school and enrolled in State School for Applied Arts, Hamburg; studied with Fritz Behnke		October: Mussolini seized power in Italy

1923–1932: EDUCATION AND INDEPENDENCE AS AN ARTIST; THE BERLIN YEARS

1923	February: moved to Berlin	
1924	Attended the private Lewin Funke Art School; studied with Willy Jaeckel	
	Winter: attended the Berlin Academy of Fine Arts until 1929; studied with Cesar Klein and Paul Plontke, later with Hans Meid	
1925		Adolf Hitler published *Mein Kampf*
1925– 1926	Met Felka Platek, an art student, in Berlin	
	Exhibits of Felka's portraiture reviewed in Berlin's Jewish periodicals	
1927	Exhibited in Berlin at the Galleries Caspar, Nierendorf, Wertheim, and at the Kunstgewerbemuseum (Applied Arts Museum)	Vandalism and anti-Semitic defacement of the Osnabrück synagogue and Jewish cemetery
1928	One-year study trip to Belgium	
1929	Set up studio as an independent artist in Berlin	New York stock market crash; beginning of the Great Depression
1931	Exhibited in Berlin, Potsdam and Dresden	
1932	Submitted for the Rome Prize of the Prussian Academy of Art	

95. Family photograph taken at Norderney, 1925

1932–1934: ROME AND ITALY, THE FIRST EXILE YEARS

1932	August: resided at Villa Massimo, Rome campus of the Prussian Academy of Art until March 1933		
	December: about 150 early works destroyed in a fire at Berlin studio		
	Cover illustrations for the magazine *Der Querschnitt*		
1933	January: last time Nussbaum's paintings appeared in the Berlin Secession Exhibit		January 30: Adolf Hitler appointed Chancellor
	March: Grant at the Villa Massimo extended until June		March 30: Dachau, the first concentration camp, opened
	End of May: fellowship withdrawn; left Villa Massimo for Alassio		April 1: boycott of more than 40 Jewish businesses in Osnabrück, including the family firm Gossels & Nussbaum
			May 10: book burnings
		September: parents traveled to Switzerland and Italy	September 22: Reichskulturkammer Law
1934	Nussbaum, Felka Platek and Nussbaum's parents in Rapallo		

1935–1940: BELGIUM, TEMPORARY ASYLUM

1935	January: traveled with Felka Platek to Belgium via Paris	Parents returned to Cologne; sold family home. Justus ran business in Osnabrück	September 15: Nuremberg Laws
	February: in Ostend with Felka Platek		
1935–1937	Moved repeatedly between Ostend and Brussels with 6-month residency permits as "resident aliens"		
1937	September: moved permanently to Brussels	July: Justus Nussbaum moved to Amsterdam	July: *Entartete Kunst* ("degenerate art") exhibition
	October 6: marriage to Felka Platek		
1937–1938	Scattered exhibitions in Ghent, Amsterdam and Paris		
1938			October 28: expulsion of Polish Jews from Germany
			November 9–10: anti-Jewish pogrom (*Kristallnacht*)
			November 10: deportation of male Jewish residents of Osnabrück to Buchenwald
1939		May: Parents fled to Amsterdam	February: St. Cyprien opened for Spanish refugees
			March 20: over 4,000 works of art burned in the courtyard of the

96. New Year's Eve party, ca. 1928

109. Prisoners at St. Cyprien (Nussbaum lying in foreground)

The Dossin barracks at Malines, ca. 1943

Refugees fleeing Germany for France, 1936

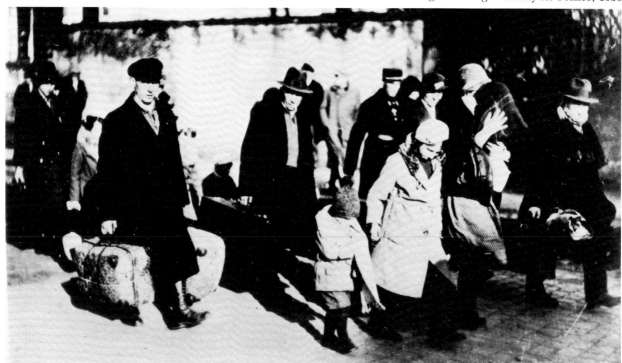

| 1939 | | | Berlin Fire Department; the works were modern in style or of Jewish authorship

September 1: beginning of World War II |

1940 INTERNMENT IN ST. CYPRIEN AND RETURN TO BRUSSELS

| 1940 | May 10: arrested in Brussels and deported to St. Cyprien, an internment camp in southern France

August 3: applied to the Kundt Commission for release

September: fled to Bordeux and returned to Brussels via Paris | | May 10: German invasion of Belgium and northern France

May 20: Auschwitz opened

May 28: Belgium surrendered

June 22: Armistice signed in France

Late October: St. Cyprien closed because of floods

October 28: registration of Belgian Jews

December 13: deportation of Osnabrück Jews to Riga and Stutthof concentration camps; most were later deported to Auschwitz |

1941–1944: LIFE IN HIDING IN BRUSSELS

| 1941 | | | October 1: forty Osnabrück Jews deported to Riga |
| 1942 | January: apartment at 22 Rue Archimède known to Gestapo; Felix and Felka sought refuge with family of sculptor Dolf Ledel

Summer: moved to attic at 22 Rue Archimède and leased cellar apartment of 23 Rue General Gratry | | January 20: Wannsee Conference; probably the decision to murder the Jews of Europe

May 27: compulsory wearing of Jewish star introduced in Belgium

June: first round-ups in Belgium

July 22: first convoy from Belgium to Auschwitz |
| 1943 | | August: parents deported to the Dutch transit camp at Westerbork | Round-up of foreign and native Jews in Amsterdam |
| 1944 | April 18: Nussbaum's last known work

July 31: last deportation train from Malines to Auschwitz; Felix and Felka Nussbaum became prisoners no. 284 and 285

August 3: the Nussbaums gassed upon arrival at Auschwitz | February: parents deported from Westerbork to Auschwitz

September 3: Justus Nussbaum deported from Westerbork to Auschwitz

Late October: Justus Nussbaum deported to Stutthof

December 7: Justus Nussbaum died at Stutthof | June 6: Allies landed at Normandy

August 15: Allies in southern France

September 3: liberation of Brussels

Late October: last gassing at Auschwitz |
| 1945 | | | January: Auschwitz liberated by the Soviet army |

CHECKLIST OF THE EXHIBITION

All works are by Felix Nussbaum, unless otherwise indicated. Height precedes width. Illustrated works are marked with an asterisk.

The following abbreviations have been used:

JZ
Junk, Peter, and Zimmer, Wendelin. *Felix Nussbaum. Leben und Werk*. Bramsche and Cologne: Rasch Verlag and DuMont Buchverlag, 1982. JZ numbers in the present checklist refer to catalogue raisonné beginning p. 210ff.

Yad Vashem Art Museum, Jerusalem
Yad Vashem: The Holocaust Martyrs' and Heroes' Remembrance Authority, The Art Museum, Jerusalem.

KMO
Kulturgeschichtliches Museum, Osnabrück.

For works included in the catalogue raisonné of Junk and Zimmer, detailed catalogue information has been omitted in the present checklist, and only additional literature has been cited.

Titles of works inscribed in the artist's hand are indicated by quotation marks.

Inscriptions have been translated into English from the original German and French; for originals, see Junk and Zimmer.

* 1. *"Remain Pious,"* 1920
   Pen, brush and ink on paper
   9$^{7/16}$ × 6$^{5/16}$" (24 × 16 cm.) / JZ 1
   Inscribed on verso:
   "Dedicated to Alfred Gossels as an everlasting reminder of his Bar Mitzvah. Felix Nussbaum 31 July 1920."
   [Gossels was Nussbaum's cousin.]
   Collection Jens Gärtner, Osnabrück

   This is Nussbaum's earliest extant work. The sixteen-year-old artist was inspired by E.M. Lilien's famous Bible illustrations for *Die Bücher der Bibel* (Berlin/Vienna, 1908).

2. *Portrait of a Young Man (Self-Portrait?)*, ca. 1925
   Oil on canvas
   25$^{3/16}$ × 15$^{3/8}$" (64 × 39 cm.) / JZ 4
   KMO

* 3. *"The Two Jews." Interior of the Osnabrück Synagogue,* 1926
   Oil on canvas
   45$^{1/4}$ × 39" (115 × 99 cm.) / JZ 6
   KMO

   In his first large painting Nussbaum depicted himself and Cantor Elias Abraham Gittelsohn as the "two Jews" in the foreground (compare No. 97). This painting hung in the clubroom of the Osnabrück synagogue on Rolandstrasse until the synagogue was destroyed by vandals during the *Kristallnacht* pogrom of November 9–10, 1938 (see No. 107). How this painting survived and the manner in which it found its way to Nussbaum in Brussels remains a mystery.

* 4. *"My Mother,"* August 1926
   Oil on canvas
   19$^{11/16}$ × 21$^{5/8}$" (50 × 55 cm.) / JZ 5
   KMO

* 5. *"Mill in East Friesland,"* 1926
   Drypoint
   3$^{5/16}$ × 5$^{1/2}$" (10 × 14 cm.) / JZ 9
   Inscribed:
   "To my dear Georg Gossels for [his] birthday. Felix. Berlin, March 1st 1927."
   Collection Uwe Gärtner, Osnabrück

6. *The Hakenhof on Kommenderiestrasse in Osnabrück,* 1927
   Oil on canvas
   14$^{3/4}$ × 13" (37.5 × 33 cm.) / JZ 21
   Collection Hans-Friedrich Janssen, West Berlin

* 7. *"Talea,"* 1927
   Oil on canvas
   39$^{3/8}$ x 23$^{5/8}$" (100 × 60 cm.) / JZ 22
   KMO

8. *"Radio Tower No. 2,"* 1928
   Oil on canvas
   23$^{7/16}$ × 14$^{15/16}$" (59.5 × 38 cm.) / JZ 34
   KMO

This depiction of one of Berlin's radio towers is an early example of Nussbaum's interest in the mechanistic apparatus of communication. Telephone wires appear frequently in his work (e.g. No. 9), and a similar radio tower appears in *Self-Portrait in a Surreal Landscape* (No. 49).

* 9. *Country Road with Felix Nussbaum Painting,* 1928
Oil on canvas
27⁵/₁₆ × 16⁹/₁₆ " (71 × 42 cm.) / JZ 35
Private Collection

The figure in the left foreground has been identified as Felix's father. An amateur painter himself, Philipp Nussbaum encouraged and financially supported his son's artistic career.

10. *Still Life with Brushes,* 1929
Pen and ink with charcoal heightened with white on brown paper
12³/₈ × 12³/₁₆ " (31.5 × 31 cm.) / JZ 60
KMO

* 11. *Memory of Norderney,* 1929
Oil on canvas
38⁹/₁₆ × 43⁵/₁₆" (98 × 110 cm.) / JZ 61
Inscribed on postcard:
"Feeling of sorrow — which is like a wheel rolling over our soul. But in spite of it, I am no spoilsport — and we are quite a merry company. So let us leave to the modern painters the things that are invisible to our eyes! For today, the most heartfelt greetings and kisses, Your [loving] son Felix."
KMO

The white building in this painting depicts the Villa Nordsee, the pension where the Nussbaums stayed while vacationing on Norderney. (See No. 15.)

* 12. *Funeral,* ca. 1930
Oil on canvas
16¹⁵/₁₆ × 14¹⁵/₁₆" (43 × 38 cm.) / JZ 66
Berlinische Galerie, Berlin

* 13. *Organ Grinder,* 1931
Oil on canvas
34⁵/₈ × 28³/₄" (88 × 73 cm.) / JZ 71
Berlinische Galerie, Berlin

* 14. *"Der tolle Platz"* (The Fantastic Square — Pariser Platz, Berlin), 1931
Oil on canvas
38³/₁₆ × 76¹⁵/₁₆" (97 × 195.5 cm.) / JZ 76
Berlinische Galerie, Berlin

* 15. *Norderney: Villa Nordsee,* July 1932
Pen and ink on paper
18¹/₂ × 22¹/₄" (47 × 56.5 cm.) / JZ 81
KMO

The Villa Nordsee was a pension on the island of Norderney where the Nussbaum family vacationed; it also appears as a motif in No. 11. (See also No. 95.)

* 16. *"Black Poodle,"* 1932
Oil on canvas
17¹¹/₁₆ × 13³/₄" (45 × 35 cm.) / JZ 79
Collection Gustel and Jaakow Moses

17. *"The Shameless Sculpture,"* 1932
Oil on canvas
25³/₁₆ × 20¹/₁₆" (64 × 51 cm.) / JZ 80
KMO

18. *Outdoor Workshop,* 1932
Pen, brush, and ink heightened with white on paper
19¹⁵/₁₆ × 13⁹/₁₆" (50.7 × 34.5 cm.) / JZ 83
Yad Vashem Art Museum, Jerusalem.
Gift of Mr. Roger D. Kats, Belgium

* 19. *Fishing Boats off Norderney,* 1932
Pen, brush, and ink heightened with white on paper
17¹¹/₁₆ × 14⁹/₁₆" (45 × 37 cm.) / JZ N7
KMO

* 20. *Wall in Rome,* 1932
Oil on canvas
15⁹/₁₆ × 22⁷/₁₆" (39.5 × 57 cm.) / JZ 86
KMO

* 21. *"Sin of the Imagination,"* 1933
Cover design for *Der Querschnitt,* no. 13 (1933), vol. 12
Offset print (original: watercolor on paper)
9⁵/₈ × 7⁵/₁₆" (24.5 × 18.5 cm.) / JZ 92
Collection Peter Junk, Osnabrück

22. *Snowman,* 1933
Cover design for *Der Querschnitt,* no. 14 (1934), vol. 2
Offset print (original: watercolor on paper)
9⁵/₈ × 7⁵/₁₆" (24.5 × 18.5 cm.) / JZ 93
Collection Wendelin Zimmer, Osnabrück

23. *Farmyard in the Roman Campagna,* 1933
Gouache and oil on paper
18¹/₈ × 23¹/₄" (46 × 59 cm.) / JZ 97
KMO

* 24. *Destruction (1),* ca. 1933
Brush and ink on paper
19¹¹/₁₆ × 27⁹/₁₆" (50 × 70 cm.) / JZ 102
KMO

* 25. *Destruction (2),* 1933
Oil on canvas
20⁷/₈ × 29¹⁵/₁₆" (53 × 76 cm.) / JZ 103
Private Collection

* 26. *White Boat in Front of a Wall,* 1933
Gouache and oil on paper
18¹/₂ × 24⁷/₁₆" (47 × 62 cm.) / JZ 112
KMO

* 27. *"Fisherman's House in Alassio,"* 1933
Gouache on paper
25$\frac{3}{8}$ × 19$\frac{1}{8}$″ (64.5 × 47.5 cm.) / JZ 119
KMO

28. *The Bay of Amalfi,* 1933
Gouache on paper
18$\frac{1}{2}$ × 25$\frac{9}{16}$″ (47 × 65 cm.) / JZ 123
KMO

* 29. *"Rapallo,"* 1934
Gouache on paper
19$\frac{7}{8}$ × 13$\frac{3}{4}$″ (50.5 × 35 cm.) / JZ 125
KMO

* 30. *"Underpass in Rapallo,"* 1934
Gouache and oil on paper
20$\frac{1}{16}$ × 14″ (51 × 35.5 cm.) / JZ 130
KMO

* 31. *"Sick Horseman"* (*Death and the Rider*), 1935
Gouache on board
25$\frac{13}{16}$ × 19$\frac{7}{8}$″ (65.5 × 50.5 cm.) / JZ 137
KMO

* 32. *The Classical Singing Lesson,* 1935
Gouache on paper
Signed and dated (lower right): Felix Nussbaum, 1935
20$\frac{1}{4}$ × 24$\frac{5}{8}$″ (51.5 × 62.5 cm.) / not in JZ
The Israel Museum, Jerusalem. Gift of Mrs. Sonia
Teikas-Steinfeld

Literature: Émile Langui, "Interviews op Mansarden.
Felix Nussbaum: de zachte humor in ballingschap,"
Vooruit. Orgaan der Belgische Werkliedenpartij, vol.
55, no. 35, 5 February 1939, p. 8 (ill.).

* 33. *"Masks and Cat"* (*Masked Self-Portrait as Painter*),
1935
Gouache on board
25$\frac{13}{16}$ × 19$\frac{7}{8}$″ (65.5 × 50.5 cm.) / JZ 139
KMO

34. *Two Masks,* 1935
Oil on canvas
26 × 18$\frac{1}{2}$″ (66 × 47 cm.) / JZ 140
Collection Dr. Andor Koritz, Berlin

* 35. *Self-Portrait with Canvas Stretcher,* 1935
Oil on canvas
24$\frac{13}{16}$ × 20$\frac{1}{16}$″ (63 × 51 cm.) / JZ 144
Collection Shulamith and Seev Jaari, Beer Tuvia, Israel

* 36. *Self-Portrait with Dishtowel,* ca. 1935
Oil on panel
25$\frac{1}{2}$ × 19$\frac{5}{8}$″ (64.8 × 49.8 cm.) / JZ 146
Collection Industrie-und Handelskammer Osnabrück

37. *Boat Mast with Ship's Lantern,* 1936
Oil on panel
24$\frac{5}{8}$ × 18$\frac{11}{16}$″ (62.5 × 47.5 cm.) / JZ 192
KMO

* 38. *Fishwife in Harbor,* 1936
Oil on panel
20 × 25$\frac{3}{4}$″ (50.8 × 65.4 cm.) / JZ 196
KMO

* 39. *Grimacing Self-Portrait with Paper Hat,* 1936
Charcoal on paper
24$\frac{13}{16}$ × 19$\frac{5}{16}$″ (63 × 49 cm.) / JZ 179
KMO

40. *Self-Portrait with Kerchief,* 1936
Charcoal on paper
24$\frac{13}{16}$ × 18$\frac{7}{8}$″ (63 × 48 cm.) / JZ 184
KMO

* 41. *Self-Portrait with Shadow,* 1936
Charcoal on paper
24$\frac{7}{16}$ × 19$\frac{5}{16}$″ (62 × 49 cm.) / JZ 186
KMO

* 42. *Masked Self-Portrait with Paper Hat and Paper Horn,*
ca. 1936
Charcoal on paper
24$\frac{13}{16}$ × 19$\frac{5}{16}$″ (63 × 49 cm.) / JZ 181
KMO

* 43. *Portrait of Felka Platek,* ca. 1936
Charcoal on paper
23$\frac{5}{8}$ × 18$\frac{7}{8}$″ (60 × 48 cm.) / JZ 189
KMO

* 44. *Self-Portrait with Brother,* 1937
Oil on panel
19$\frac{7}{8}$ × 25$\frac{3}{4}$″ (50.5 × 65.4 cm.) / JZ 207
KMO

* 45. *Man at the Window* (*Self-Portrait after Adriaen van
Ostade*), 1937
Oil on panel
25$\frac{13}{16}$ × 19$\frac{15}{16}$″ (65.5 × 50.6 cm.) / JZ 210
KMO

46. *Don Quixote and the Windmills,* 1938
Oil on panel
25$\frac{9}{16}$ × 19$\frac{11}{16}$″ (65 × 50 cm.) / JZ 212
Collection Dr. Andor Koritz, Berlin

* 47. *Still Life with Barred Window,* 1938
Oil on canvas
24$\frac{13}{16}$ × 21$\frac{7}{16}$″ (63 × 54.5 cm.) / JZ 215
KMO

48. *Self-Portrait with an Appleblossom*, 1939
Oil on canvas
29³/₄ × 24¹⁵/₁₆″ (75.5 × 63.4 cm.) / JZ 224
Collection Gustel and Jaakow Moses

* 49. *Self-Portrait in a Surreal Landscape*, ca. 1939
Oil on panel
25³/₈ × 19³/₄″ (64.4 × 50.2 cm.) / JZ 221
Collection Shulamith and Seev Jaari, Beer Tuvia, Israel

* 50. *Couple in a Surreal Landscape*, ca. 1939
Oil on panel
19¹⁵/₁₆ × 25¹³/₁₆″ (50.6 × 65.6 cm.) / JZ 222
KMO

* 51. *Self-Portrait in the Studio*, ca. 1939
Gouache on paper
24⁷/₁₆ × 18⁷/₈″ (62 × 48 cm.) / JZ 226
KMO

* 52. *Mummenschanz (Masquerade)*, ca. 1939
Oil on canvas
28³/₄ × 38⁹/₁₆″ (73 × 98 cm.) / JZ 227
The David and Alfred Smart Gallery, The University of Chicago, Chicago, Illinois. Gift of Mr. and Mrs. Eugene Davidson, Dr. and Mrs. Edwin DeCosta, Mr. and Mrs. Gaylord Donnelley, and Mrs. Harold T. Martin

* 53. *European Vision*, 1939
Oil on canvas
23⁵/₈ × 29¹/₈″ (60 × 74 cm.) / JZ 228
Collection Gustel and Jaakow Moses

* 54. *The Secret (1)*, 1939
Pencil and gouache on paper
Image: 6¹/₈ × 7¹¹/₁₆″ (15.5 × 19.5 cm.)
Sheet: 9⁵/₈ × 12³/₁₆″ (24.5 × 31 cm.) / JZ 229
KMO

* 55. *"The Secret" (2)*, November 1939
Oil on canvas
24 × 29⁵/₁₆″ (61 × 74.5 cm.) / JZ 230
Private Collection

* 56. *View of Rooftops in Brussels (Gloves)*, 1940
Gouache on paper
25⁹/₁₆ × 20¹/₄″ (65 × 51.5 cm.) / JZ 237
Yad Vashem Art Museum, Jerusalem. Gift of Mr. Roger D. Kats, Belgium

57. *Still Life with Glove*, ca. 1940
Gouache on paper
Signed (upper right): Felix Nussbaum
17¹¹/₁₆ × 23¹³/₁₆″ (45 × 60.5 cm.) / not in JZ
Yad Vashem Art Museum, Jerusalem.
Gift of Mr. Roger D. Kats, Belgium

* 58. *Studio in Brussels*, 1940
Gouache on paper
24⁷/₁₆ × 18⁷/₈″ (62 × 48 cm.) / JZ 238
KMO

* 59. *Still Life with Lay Figure*, ca. 1940
Oil on canvas
39³/₈ × 34⁵/₈″ (100 × 88 cm.) / JZ 243
Collection Gustel and Jaakow Moses

* 60. *Portrait of Felka Platek*, 1940
Gouache and charcoal on paper
27¹⁵/₁₆ × 20⁷/₈″ (71 × 53 cm.) / JZ 245
KMO

61. *Huddled Man*, ca. 1940
Charcoal, chalk, gouache, and pen and ink on brown paper
16³/₄ × 12³/₈ ″ (42.5 × 31.5 cm.) / JZ 265
KMO

62. *Prisoners at St. Cyprien (1)*, ca. 1940
Pencil on tracing paper
Image: 7⁷/₈ × 15³/₈ ″ (20 × 39 cm.)
Sheet: 10⁵/₈ × 17¹¹/₁₆ ″ (27 × 45 cm.) / JZ 248
KMO

* 63. *Prisoners at St. Cyprien (2)*, 1940
Pencil and watercolor on paper
11⁵/₈ × 18¹/₈ ″ (29.5 × 46 cm.) / JZ 249
Inscribed (lower left): "Study for a painting";
(lower right): "Dedicated in friendship to my dear Weichmann family"
Leo Baeck Institute, New York

64. *The Camp Synagogue (1)*, 1940
Pen, brush, ink, and pencil on paper
7¹/₂ × 11⁷/₁₆ ″ (19 × 29 cm.) / JZ 250
KMO

* 65. *The Camp Synagogue (2)*, 1941
Oil on panel
19¹¹/₁₆ × 25¹/₂ ″ (50 × 64.7 cm.) / JZ 251
Yad Vashem Art Museum, Jerusalem. Gift of the Freund Family, Jerusalem

Literature: Yad Vashem — Martyrs' and Heroes' Remembrance Authority Art Museum. *Testimony: Art of the Holocaust*. Jerusalem: 1982. Cover ill.

66. *Fear (Self-Portrait with Niece Marianne)*, 1941
Oil on canvas
20¹/₁₆ × 15⁹/₁₆ ″ (51 × 39.5 cm.) / JZ 253
Collection Shulamith and Seev Jaari, Beer Tuvia, Israel

* 67. *Despairing Women*, 1941
Pencil on tracing paper
8¹¹/₁₆ × 7¹/₁₆ ″ (22 × 18 cm.) / JZ 254
KMO

* 68. *Weeping Woman*, 1941
Oil on panel
20½ × 18⅞ " (52 × 48 cm.) / JZ 257
Collection Shulamith and Seev Jaari, Beer Tuvia, Israel

69. *Woman and Girl ("Study for a Painting")*, 1941
Pencil on tracing paper
Image: 5⅛ × 5⅞ " (13 × 15 cm.)
Sheet: 5⁹⁄₁₆ × 6½ " (14 × 16.5 cm.) / JZ 258
KMO

70. *Young Couple*, 1941
Oil on canvas
34⅝ × 28⅛ " (88 × 71.5 cm.) / JZ 259
KMO

* 71. *Loneliness*, 1942
Oil on canvas
37⅜ × 24" (95 × 61 cm.) / JZ 262
Private Collection, Osnabrück

72. *Man in a Tree*, 5 March 1942
Pencil and charcoal on paper
14³⁄₁₆ × 10⅝" (36 × 27 cm.) / JZ 264
KMO

Nussbaum inscribed this view from his studio window into the back courtyard with the date and address: "Brussels, 22 rue Archimède."

* 73. *Prisoners at St. Cyprien (3)*, 1942
Oil on canvas
26⁹⁄₁₆ × 53¹⁵⁄₁₆" (67.5 × 137 cm.) / JZ 266
Inscribed on verso:
"Felix Nussbaum ST. CYPRIEN (unfinished) 18 June 1942"
KMO

* 74. *Group Portrait*, 1942
Oil on canvas
20¹⁄₁₆ × 31¹¹⁄₁₆" (51 × 80.5 cm.) / JZ 267
Private Collection, Osnabrück

The man holding an acacia leaf at lower right is a self-portrait.

* 75. *"Soir" (Self-Portrait with Felka Platek)*, June 1942
Oil on canvas
34¼ × 28⅜" (87 × 72 cm.) / JZ 268
Inscribed on verso:
"SOIR (unfinished) June 1942 Felix Nussbaum"
KMO

76. *Gymnasts*, ca. 1942
Ceramic tile, painted and fired
5⅞ × 5⅞" (15 × 15 cm.) / not in JZ
Signed (lower right): Felix
Collection Brigitte Junk, Hasbergen

The motif is taken from an oil painting of 1929 (JZ 54) that was presumably destroyed in the fire in Nussbaum's Berlin studio in 1932. Nussbaum produced small

painted ceramics (see also No. 77 and pitcher depicted in No. 83) to support himself while in exile and hiding.

77. *Boat Mast*, ca. 1943
Etched glass tile
7⅞ × 7⅞" (20 × 20 cm.) / JZ 193
KMO

The decoration of this tile is an adaptation of No. 37.

* 78. *Mannequins*, 1943
Oil on canvas
39⅜ × 32⁵⁄₁₆" (100 × 82 cm.) / JZ 269
KMO

* 79. *The Kitchen in Hiding*, 20 March 1943
Pen and ink with charcoal on paper
18⅞ × 25³⁄₁₆" (48 × 64 cm.) / JZ 271
KMO

* 80. *View from the Studio Window*, March 1943
Pen, brush and ink, gouache on blue-gray paper
12⅝ × 15¾" (31 × 39 cm.) / JZ 272
KMO

81. *Still Life with Bottle and Pitchers*, 23 March 1943
Pencil and charcoal on paper
14¾ × 11¹³⁄₁₆" (37.5 × 30 cm.) / JZ 273
KMO

* 82. *Still Life with Egg*, March 1943
Gouache on paper
14⁹⁄₁₆ × 12⅜" (37 × 31.5 cm.) / JZ 274
KMO

* 83. *Still Life with Doll and Tennis Racquet*, June 1943
Oil on canvas
22¹⁄₁₆ × 18⅞" (56 × 48 cm.) / JZ 275
KMO

* 84. *Organ Grinder*, July 1943
Oil on canvas
39 × 32⁵⁄₁₆" (99 × 82 cm.) / JZ 276
Inscribed on verso:
"ORGAN PLAYER (unfinished) June 1942"
KMO

Nussbaum left this work unfinished in June 1942 (along with Nos. 73 and 75), and only completed it the following July.

* 85. *Self-Portrait at the Easel*, August 1943
Oil on canvas
29½ × 21⅝" (75 × 55 cm.) / JZ 277
KMO

* 86. *Self-Portrait with Jewish Identity Card*, probably late 1943
Oil on canvas
21⅝ × 18⅞" (55 × 48 cm.) / JZ 278
KMO

Literature: Roters, Eberhard, *et al. Berlin 1910–1933.*
New York: Rizzoli, 1982, p. 132, ill. (color), fig. 136.

* 87. *Grieving Couple,* 6 December 1943
Oil on canvas
24⁷/₁₆ × 19⁵/₁₆″ (62 × 49 cm.) / JZ 280
KMO

* 88. *The Damned (1),* ca. 1943
Pencil on paper
4¹⁵/₁₆ × 8¼″ (12.5 × 21 cm.) / JZ 281
Inscribed in right margin:
"Gas lamps" "Skeletons"
KMO

* 89. *The Damned (2),* 1943 / 5 January 1944
Oil on canvas
39¾ × 60¼″ (101 × 153 cm.) / JZ 282
KMO

* 90. *Jaqui on the Street,* late January 1944
Oil on panel (partially perforated)
27¾ × 19⁵/₁₆″ (70.5 × 49 cm.) / JZ 283
KMO

91. *Study for a Painting: The Skeletons Play for a Dance,*
ca. 1944
Pencil on paper
8¼ × 11¹³/₁₆″ (21 × 30 cm.) / JZ 284
KMO

* 92. *Skeletons Playing Musical Instruments* (preparatory
drawing for *The Skeletons Play for a Dance*), ca. 1944
Pencil and gouache on brown paper
13³/₁₆ × 8⁷/₈″ (33.5 × 22.5 cm.) / JZ 285
KMO

* 93. *The Skeletons Play for a Dance,* 18 April 1944
Oil on canvas
39³/₈ × 59¹/₁₆″ (100 × 150 cm.) / JZ 286
KMO

This is Felix Nussbaum's last-known work.

DOCUMENTS

94. Facade of Felix Nussbaum's birthplace.
March 1880. Pen and ink on linen-paper
Collection Stadt Osnabrück — Bauordnungsamt-Archiv,
Osnabrück

* 95. Family photograph taken on the occasion of the Silver
Wedding Anniversary of Philipp and Rahel Nussbaum,
Norderney, 29 May 1925, with their sons, Felix and
Justus.
KMO

* 96. New Year's Eve party.
Photograph, ca. 1928
KMO

Felix Nussbaum is seated in the left foreground; his
brother, Justus, is the second from the right.

97. a) Interior of the synagogue on Rolandstrasse, Osna-
brück.
b) Cantor Elias Abraham Gittelsohn in the synagogue.
Photographs, 1928
Collection Lori Gittelson, New Rochelle, N.Y.
See No. 3.

98. Advertisement for the Nussbaum Family Business:
"Gossels & Co., Ironworks, Osnabrück, Supplier of all
Iron, Tin, Pipes, Implements, and Hardware."
Berlin-Halensee: DARI Verlag, 1928
Collection Stadtbibliothek Osnabrück

99. Felix Nussbaum's letter of application for the *Rompreis*
stipend at the German Academy (Villa Massimo) in
Rome. Osnabrück, 24 March 1932.
Collection Akademie der Künste, Archiv
der Preussischen Akademie der Künste, Berlin

The letter lists the five works Nussbaum submitted to
the competition for the Academy's Rome fellowship
(*Rompreis*), including Nos. 14, 16 and 17 in this exhibition. Though Nussbaum did not obtain the *Rompreis,*
he did receive a grant of free room and studio space at
the Villa Massimo.

100. Administrative buildings of the German Academy, Villa
Massimo, Rome.
Photograph, Luigi Leoni, Rome, ca. 1930
Collection Deutsche Akademie Villa Massimo, Rome

101. National Socialist Poster for the Reichstag Election on 5
March 1933: "Marxism is the Guardian Angel of Capital-
ism. Vote for the National Socialists."
Collection Bundesarchiv, Koblenz

102. *Osnabrücker Tageblatt* (Osnabrück Daily News), 1 April
1933. Front page with headline calling for a boycott of
Jewish business establishments.
Collection Niedersächsisches Staatsarchiv, Osnabrück

103. Josef Goebbels and his wife, Magda, during their first
visit to Italy in May 1933, inspecting the Foro Mussolini
in Rome.
Photograph, 1933
KMO

104. Letter of Felix Nussbaum to Professor Herbert
Gericke, director of the German Academy in Rome.
Alassio, 11 June 1933
Collection Deutsche Akademie Villa Massimo, Rome

Nussbaum wrote to Gericke asking the director to send
him some paintings he had left behind in Rome owing
to the "circumstances of" his "sudden departure."
Nussbaum also refers to a novel he was writing, which
has yet to be found.

* 105. Alien registration card issued to Felix Nussbaum on 16 November 1935; renewed on 16 November 1937.
KMO

The French inscription, hand-written in red ink in the left-hand margin, reads: "The bearer of this certificate is bound, on pain of immediate expulsion from the realm, to undertake no employment in Belgium."

106. Store of Samson and David in Osnabrück, after the looting during the *Kristallnacht* pogrom of 9–10 November 1938.
Photograph, Karl Ordelheide, 1938
Collection Karl Ordelheide, Osnabrück

107. The destroyed synagogue on Rolandstrasse, Osnabrück.
Photograph, Karl Ordelheide, 1938
Collection Karl Ordelheide, Osnabrück

108. Registration of Felix Nussbaum at the internment camp of St. Cyprien.
Reproduction
Courtesy of Archives de Préfecture des Pyrénées-Atlantiques, Pau. KMO

* 109. Group photograph of prisoners in the internment camp of St. Cyprien.
Photograph, J.R. Emmel, 1940
KMO

Felix Nussbaum is lying in the foreground.

* 110. "The Prisoners at St. Cyprien"
Photo-essay in *Zürcher Illustrierte*, no. 47, 22 November 1940, pp. 1288–89 (reproduction).
Courtesy of Ringier Dokumentationszentrum, Zurich

111. Law concerning measures against Jews, including legal and social restrictions requiring Jewish registration.
Issued by the German Military Headquarters in Belgium and northern France, 28 October 1940.
Reproduction
Collection Bundesarchiv (Militärarchiv), Freiburg

112. Registration of Felix Nussbaum as a Jew, Brussels, 24 December 1940, indicating that he had automatically lost his German citizenship by living abroad, under the terms of the Eleventh Decree of the German Citizenship Law, 25 November 1941.
KMO

113. Decree ordering Jews to wear the yellow star.
Issued by the German Military Headquarters in Belgium and northern France, 27 May 1942.
Reproduction
Collection, Bundesarchiv (Militärarchiv), Freiburg

114. Passport photograph of Felix Nussbaum, dated 26 June 1942.
KMO

115. Apartment of Felix and Felka Nussbaum on the second floor of 22 Rue Archimède in Brussels.
Sketch by Christian Jacque, Brussels, 1983
KMO

116. Corner house with grocery store on Rue Archimède in Brussels.
Photograph, Eugène Etienne, Brussels, ca. 1935
KMO

The photographer Eugène Etienne resided at 22 Rue Archimède, where the Nussbaums lived in hiding. Etienne reports that Nussbaum and his wife ventured out to purchase groceries at the store, which is visible in the background of *Soir (Self-Portrait with Felka Platek* — No. 75).

117. Order for Felix Nussbaum and Felka Platek to report for compulsory labor assignment, issued 21 June 1944.
KMO

"Compulsory labor assignment" was often a euphemism for deportation to the east.

118. Arrival of Jewish prisoners at the Dossin barracks in the transit camp at Malines.
Photograph, Maurice Pioro, Brussels, 1943
KMO

LENDERS

Akademie der Künste,
    Archiv der Preussischen Akademie der Künste, Berlin
Bauordnungsamt-Archiv Stadt Osnabrück
Berlinische Galerie, Berlin
Bundesarchiv (Militärarchiv), Freiburg
Bundesarchiv, Koblenz
The David and Alfred Smart Gallery,
    The University of Chicago, Chicago, Illinois
Deutsche Akademie Villa Massimo, Rome
Jens Gärtner, Osnabrück
Uwe Gärtner, Osnabrück
Lori Gittelson, New Rochelle, N.Y.
The Israel Museum, Jerusalem
Shulamith and Seev Jaari, Beer Tuvia, Israel
Hans-Friedrich Janssen, Berlin
Brigitte Junk, Hasbergen
Peter Junk, Osnabrück
Dr. Andor Koritz, Berlin
Kulturgeschichtliches Museum, Osnabrück
Leo Baeck Institute, New York
Gustel and Jaakow Moses
Niedersächsisches Staatsarchiv, Osnabrück
Karl Ordelheide, Osnabrück
Stadtbibliothek Osnabrück
Yad Vashem Art Museum, Jerusalem
Private Collections (2)

PHOTOGRAPHY

Hartwig Fender: Nos. 1, 4, 5, 73, 84, 87
E. Harms: No. 55
Kurt Löckmann: Nos. 3, 36, 90, 93
Eric Pollitzer: No. 63
Foto Strenger: Nos. 11, 21, 25, 38, 43, 58, 75, 78, 79, 83, 85,
    86, 88, 89
Baruch Rimon: Nos. 56, 65
De Chirico, p. 54: The Museum of Modern Art, New York,
    Nelson A. Rockefeller Bequest
De Chirico, p. 57: The Museum of Modern Art, New York,
    James Thrall Soby Bequest
St. Cyprien, pp. 76 and 79: courtesy
    Ringierdokumentationszentrum, Zurich
Jewish refugees, p. 86: courtesy Joint Distribution
    Committee, New York
Barracks at Malines, p. 86: Centre Documentation Juive
    Contemporaine, Paris